Nature and Culture
in the
Early Modern
Atlantic

THE EARLY MODERN AMERICAS

Peter C. Mancall, Series Editor

Volumes in the series explore neglected aspects of early
modern history in the western hemisphere. Interdisciplinary
in character, and with a special emphasis on the Atlantic World
from 1450 to 1850, the series is published in partnership with
the USC-Huntington Early Modern Studies Institute.

PETER C. MANCALL

Nature and Culture in the Early Modern Atlantic

PENN

University of Pennsylvania Press

Philadelphia

Publication of this volume was aided by generous grants from the Andrew W. Mellon Foundation and from Furthermore: a program of the J. M. Kaplan Fund.

Furthermore:
a program of the J.M. Kaplan Fund

Published by
University of Pennsylvania Press
Philadelphia, Pennsylvania 19104-4112
www.upenn.edu/pennpress

Printed in the United States of America on acid-free paper

1 3 5 7 9 10 8 6 4 2

Library of Congress Cataloging-in-Publication Data
Names: Mancall, Peter C., author.
Title: Nature and culture in the early modern Atlantic / Peter C. Mancall.
Other titles: Early modern Americas.
Description: 1st edition. | Philadelphia : University of Pennsylvania Press,
    [2018] | Series: The early modern Americas | Includes bibliographical
    references and index.
Identifiers: LCCN 2017026864 | ISBN 9780812249668 (hardcover : alk.
    paper)
Subjects: LCSH: Atlantic Ocean Region—History—16th century. | Nature and
    civilization—Atlantic Ocean Region—History—16th century. | Philosophy
    of nature—Europe—History—16th century. | Philosophy of nature—North
    America—History—16th century. | Indian philosophy—North America. |
    America—Discovery and exploration.
Classification: LCC D210 .M29 2018 | DDC 304.209182/109031—dc23
LC record available at https://lccn.loc.gov/2017026864

In memory of
Elliott
(1927–2013)
and Jackie
(1932–2013)

CONTENTS

PREFACE

This book is about humans and nature in the sixteenth-century Atlantic basin. At its heart lies a selection of images, namely, a set of painted panels from a fourteenth-century cloister in a cathedral in the south of France, an illustrated manuscript atlas assembled at Dieppe on the Normandy coast in 1547, a manuscript of uncertain provenance from the late sixteenth-century Caribbean and coastal America, and English and northern European depictions of coastal Carolina in 1585 and 1590. Such visual evidence, among the abundant illustrative material in printed books and hand-painted codices, reveals early modern ecological thinking among Europeans and the indigenous residents of the Western Hemisphere. In the sixteenth century, as now, everyone thought about nature. Europeans and indigenous Americans alike devised ways to understand and take advantage of what the English natural historian Edward Topsell called in the early seventeenth century the "troublesome and vast Ocean of Natures admirable fabricature."[1] But views of nature did not remain static. Instead, ecological sensibilities shifted over the course of the century when the peoples around the basin incorporated new information into their understanding of nature—evidence produced from the increasing number of journeys back and forth across the ocean. Put another way, new knowledge of nature produced a shift in the nature of knowledge—in this case, how individuals understood changing environments.

The three main chapters in this short book began as the Mellon Distinguished Lectures in the Humanities at the University of Pennsylvania. I have since added a postscript and a note on sources. My goal in this extended essay is twofold. First, I explicate European and indigenous American interpretations of nature and trace the ways that the natural world and human communities evolved as a result of contact between the so-called Old and New Worlds. I begin with a chapter on early modern Americans' and Europeans' capacious sense of the extent of nature around 1500, which included invisible forces and monstrous creatures. In the second chapter, I trace changes in the natural world of the basin as a result of trans-oceanic encounters. In the third chapter, I focus on the outer banks of modern North Carolina, a place so well documented that it has become a synecdoche to represent all of early North America in many historians' works. In the postscript, I describe and analyze two sixteenth-century texts about insects, one produced in Mexico and the other in Europe. I use the Note on Sources at the end to set the images and texts that are central to the main chapters into the context of writing about the environment in the early modern world.

Part of my inquiry is epistemological: how did people know what they knew about the natural world before 1600? To explore those sensibilities, I pay close attention to the range of available evidence, much of which is not found in traditional written sources. This leads to my second goal in these essays. To understand the environmental history of the sixteenth-century Atlantic basin, scholars must consider the wide range of potentially relevant evidence. So while I draw on traditional sources, such as early modern European printed books produced by travelers and natural historians, I am equally concerned with the kinds of evidence that have come to us through oral history and visual images. These bodies of knowledge have played too scant a role in scholars' exploration of the initial encounter between peoples in the basin and, more important, the impact of myriad subsequent encounters. Historians analyzing images and texts have done brilliant work in limning the relationship between peoples but an insufficient job so far of putting these human meetings into the physical context of a rapidly changing natural world. Further, I integrate insights from folklore and oral history to demonstrate the utility of sources used by scholars in some contexts (for example, historical writings informed by anthropological analysis) but, to date, less frequently in works of environmental and early modern Atlantic history. The natural world existed apart from humans' understanding of it, but every effort to explain its workings drew on culture in the broadest sense. Following from that notion, I draw on texts, images, folklore, and oral history since all can be mined to understand the relationship between nature and culture.

The chapters that follow reveal a shift in ecological sensibilities from the time of the Columbian voyages to the dawn of the seventeenth century. Historians of science in Europe have already pointed to the period from 1500 to 1700 as a period of transition, a time when explanations of the natural world that pivoted on religious explanations gave way to a more naturalistic or secular mode of explanation, although the transition was not evident at all times, multiple perspectives coexisted, and premodern attitudes did not disappear entirely even as late as the Enlightenment.[2] From this vantage point, a monster, to take one notable example, could be understood at the start of the period as a sign or a punishment from a supreme being (typically the Judeo-Christian God for most Europeans), but by 1700, that same species or specimen could be described as an oddity of nature and hence explained without recourse to divine intervention. Yet at the end of the sixteenth century, at the approximate midpoint of this larger transition, European readers could find both secular and godly explanations for natural phenomena that did not fit into defined categories of what constituted the normal.

What had prompted the move from an ages-old way of looking at nature as the product of a divine creation to a newer naturalistic perspective? Any complex shift in the ways that people understand fundamental phenomena invariably draws from multiple sources and reflects local circumstances, including alterations in economic practices, political regimes, and technological changes. But in this instance, the changes in understanding nature likely lie in the emergence of an Atlantic community in which far-flung peoples came into contact with strangers and new objects. When Europeans and Americans met each other, they exchanged much—plants and goods and animals, among other things. They also shared knowledge, about both the seen and the unseen. Europeans, who left the vast majority of written sources, often mocked indigenous Americans' spiritual beliefs. But there were more similarities between peoples on either side of the basin than some European explorers or their chroniclers might have wanted to admit.

Thoughtful observers knew that these transatlantic encounters, which took place on every level from the microscopic to the theological, prompted alterations in conceptions of nature and strategies for representing it. The physical world changed as the result of the movement of biota. But interior thoughts evolved, too. While it might push the evidence too far to suggest that the meeting of Atlantic peoples prompted the emergence of a basin-wide modern, post-providential sensibility in which nature could always be explained without recourse to divine intervention, surviving written, visual, and oral evidence at least suggests that multiple encounters across the ocean played a decisive role in what the literary scholar Stephen Greenblatt aptly called "the swerve," the shift in awareness from a medieval world (on both sides of the Atlantic) to a modern one.[3]

In the chapters that follow, I describe a narrative with two strands. On one hand, as historians have known since the pioneering work of Alfred Crosby Jr. almost a half-century ago, the movement of people and biota reshaped human and nonhuman communities across the basin, especially in the Americas, where the devastating impact of Old World infectious disease and the consequences of the arrival of European fauna was already evident by 1600.[4] As the environmental historian Donald Worster has noted, Europeans' appropriation of the natural resources of the Americas "touched off a multifaceted revolution in society, economy, politics, and culture, which swept the entire globe."[5] On the other hand, there were changes in perceptions about nature, which developed as a result of the real-world changes precipitated by exchange of physical objects and by human understanding of these changes. In Mexico in 1576, to take one notable example, Nahua artists who had likely studied a copy of Pliny's *Naturalis Historia* in the library of the Real Colegio de Santa Cruz in Tlatelolco embraced his ideas in their depictions of indigenous plants at a time when an epidemic was reducing the Mexican population by perhaps 50 percent, thereby creating a memorial to their world in a visual language used by early modern Europeans to explain phenomena known in ancient Rome.[6] Environmental change, such incidents suggest, drove psychological revolution well before the English established themselves on the banks of the James River in 1607.

Since European historians have often described the confessional wars that drove violence across the continent in the sixteenth century, I will begin with three different kinds of confession. First, much of what follows comes from sources left by Europeans. There is much here about indigenous Americans' views of nature, but the majority of it—including the insights from the Mexican codex that describes insects—survives through the intervention of Europeans. As a result, readers must be aware that these sources may be doubly mediated. Every source betrays the biases of its creator and those who have found ways to preserve and circulate the knowledge it contains. Early European viewers of Americans, keen as they might have been to transcribe what they saw or heard accurately, also had to wrestle with the unspoken assumptions that guide anyone's description of another. Their descriptions reflected their own understanding of the physical world. As a result, their writings often included comparisons between what they observed in new locales and what they and their readers knew from their homelands. Such analogous readings went beyond descriptions of nature and became ubiquitous in European works about the Americas in the sixteenth century. Second, this book about the Atlantic world pays little attention to Africa, although in places I incorporate observations about West Africa and the movement of African plants across the ocean. (I review the existing literature about the sixteenth-century environmental history of Africa in the Note on Sources.) Third, while I draw on indigenous American oral history, I do so through printed versions of knowledge once transmitted orally, rather than through gathering oral history on my own. I take this position after spending time with indigenous peoples in both the United States and New Zealand and with the full awareness that those who receive oral knowledge are not necessarily entitled to disseminate it. While it is true that written versions of narratives might reflect earlier chroniclers' indifference to cultural norms, I accept the notion that oral knowledge exists only through the act of telling and that written versions of stories once told are instead approximations of culturally protected memories. I expand on my use of oral history in the Note on Sources, where I also make suggestions for how to use underutilized written (manuscript and print) and visual sources to write a more comprehensive environmental history of the Atlantic basin in the sixteenth century.

Nature and Culture
in the
Early Modern
Atlantic

CHAPTER ONE

The Boundaries of Nature

Monsters swam, climbed, walked, and flew in the Atlantic basin in the sixteenth century. Real monsters, or at least they seemed real in the opinion of those who described them, could be found everywhere. Native peoples in the Orinoco basin told the English explorer Sir Walter Ralegh (Raleigh) that if he peered into the woods, he could encounter creatures with faces in the middle of their chests and eventually come upon a city of Amazons.[1] European cartographers, after reading the works of cosmographers, squeezed *monstra marina* into almost every open space on their maps.[2] One renowned French surgeon depicted specimens who seemed part human and part animal and provided clinical explanations for how such creatures came to exist.[3] Time and again, the monstrous stare out from an early modern page, invading our imaginations and making us wonder why people half a millennium ago thought so often about them.[4]

Europeans did not need to sail out into the Atlantic to encounter the monstrous. By the time Christopher Columbus set sail in 1492, they already possessed deep knowledge about the monsters that purportedly roamed far away, primarily to the east and the south.[5] Texts and images of nonhuman creatures had circulated since Antiquity, dating back at least to the fourth century BCE. Even

FIGURE 1. Dutch cartographers produced many of the most influential maps of the Atlantic basin in the sixteenth century. Among them was Abraham Ortelius, who created an atlas of the world drawn from various authorities. This map of Iceland in his *Theatrum Orbis Terrarum*, first published in Antwerp in 1570, depicted its famed fjords, already long explored by Norse sailors, as well as the fierce denizens that swam off its shores, seemingly patrolling the border of the scarcely peopled island. Wikimedia Commons.

scripture contained multiple references to marvels and otherworldly entities.[6] Details about monstrous creatures circulated in reports by the physician Ktesias from Knidos, who worked in the Persian court, and Megasthenes, a Greek ambassador who took up residence in modern Patna, on the Ganges, after the military expansionary campaigns of Alexander the Great. The geographers and ethnologists of the ancient world collected such reports and republished them, including Strabo, Diodorus Siculus, and especially Pliny, who completed his massive natural history in 77 CE. Monsters also appeared prominently in the works of early Christian authors such as the third-century encyclopedist Solinus and the *Etymologiae of Isadore*, written in the first half of the seventh century. Images of monsters copied from classical texts can be found in eleventh-century manuscripts.[7] They proliferated during the medieval period, primarily in the analytical category known as "wonders."[8] Churchgoers could see carvings of them in local shrines along pilgrimages, even at remote outposts such as the Priory of Serrabone, secluded in the hills of the Aspres range not far from the modern border between France and Spain. Dog-headed cynocephali appeared at Vézelay, a major pilgrimage site in Burgundy, and churchgoers across the continent walked by monstrous creatures carved into columns while gargoyles stared down on Parisians from the roofline at Notre Dame.[9]

Did Europeans who saw such representations of ludicrous and terrifying beings believe that such creatures existed? Perhaps not. Lucretius, writing in the last century before the Common Era, understood that belief in the monstrous was widespread. But he contended that such entities occurred only in the mind, not in reality. "For certainly no image of a Centaur comes from one living," he wrote in *On the Nature of Things*, "since there never was a living thing of this nature," which explained the absence of a real-world Cerberus, or light-withholding Furies, or a Tartarus "belching horrible fires from this throat," or a Scylla that was half-fish and half-dog, or a Chimera with the head of a lion, the body of a goat, and the hind parts of a serpent. None of these things could exist, he was certain, because there was no possible explanation for how they could come into being.[10]

But knowledge of Lucretius's ideas almost entirely disappeared for the next millennium and hence could not have halted the spread of visual iconography of the monstrous, which appeared with regularity in bestiaries and church carvings.[11] Similar images began to appear with ever-greater frequency in books, too.[12] Konrad of Megenberg's *Buch der Natur*, written in the mid-fourteenth century, circulated in multiple manuscripts (many still preserved) and appeared in print first in 1475 (and was reprinted five more times before the turn of the next century). The long unpaginated text contained multiple woodcuts of the prosaic aspects of nature, such as insects, flowers, and fish. It also contained representations of the monstrous—including mermaids, a chicken with a crown, a creature that had the head of a man, the body of a large feline, and wings, winged horses, and a creature with the body of a mammal, the tail of a fish, and the head of a tonsured monk.[13] By the fourteenth century, scribes had also circulated important manuscripts, such as St. Lambert of Omer's twelfth-century *Liber Floridus*, which similarly included the monstrous as well as representations of divine judgments.[14] Manuscript news of the monstrous spread across Europe, recycling ideas earlier propagated by Pliny.[15]

In the town of Fréjus in the south of France, local legend tells that the bishop ordered everyone attending mass to enter the church through its cloister. If this is true, then the parishioners had regular, perhaps weekly, encounters with a provocative series of images painted on wooden panels slotted into the cloister ceilings. The location of the images makes it difficult to see them clearly, since they perch about twelve feet above the floor. Still, after almost seven centuries, the surviving paintings (some have faded almost entirely) still attract the gaze. They evoke a moment when the boundaries between the known world and the unknown constituted a topic of active discussion in the churches, streets, libraries, and courts of Europe—and, indeed, across much of the Atlantic basin.

The cloister at Fréjus offers us a chance to consider the relationship between physical environments and human cultures in the early modern era. Its images reveal a time when there were porous

FIGURE 2. Depictions of the monstrous could be found in churches across Europe before the sixteenth century. These pictures constitute a small minority of the scores of images that survive from the fourteenth-century commission to decorate the cloister in the cathedral at Fréjus. Photo by the author. (See Plate 1.)

borders between the natural world, which earlier Europeans could understand and examine, and the other, less visible worlds that early modern peoples also believed to exist simultaneously. Those worlds included, as one eighteenth-century scholar (writing about North America) called it, the "*païs des ames*," or the country of the souls.[16] Nature hosted monsters that roamed forests and seas and occasionally threatened humans. It boasted wonders and prodigies, apparent signs of divine favor or disgust. Nature also offered manifestations of the divine, sometimes in the form of animal spirits that controlled the movements of game or in the guise of an invisible saint who interceded with God on behalf of humans. The clambering chaos of the surviving images at Fréjus—with centaurs, serpents, griffons, and dragons interspersed among mundane images—suggests that the conceptual boundaries of premodern Europeans' consciousness were mutable, imperfect, and flexible. Similarly, while no one in Europe would have known it, Americans too had created images of what would now be seen as the monstrous, the grotesque, or the supernatural. Fantastic creatures were not just figments of one's imagination or a familiar literary trope. They were part of the real world, even if they were invisible or existed only in the stories told from an alleged eyewitness to credulous listeners.

Fréjus sits along the Mediterranean about halfway between Cannes and St. Tropez. Greek traders settled there, followed by Romans, who built the port of Forum Iulii, the market of Julius Caesar. Earlier generations of scholars were consumed with the imperial and late Antique remains of the Roman town. Only a century ago, a historian could write an entire history of the old church there, now the Cathédrale Saint-Léonce, famous for its elegant fifth-century baptistery, without even mentioning the fourteenth-century cloister and the spectacular paintings that cover its ceilings.[17] After its port silted, Fréjus became a quiet town and its religious architecture was little known, although in the early seventeenth century Jacques Maretz, a mathematician on the faculty of the university at Aix-en-Provence, included a bird's-eye depiction of the town in his map of the coast of Provence.[18]

The painted panels of the cloister ceiling in Fréjus stand in stark contrast to the rest of the stone edifice. These once-brightly painted boards have suffered from the elements over time, but of the 1,235 original panels slotted into the wood ceilings, it is still possible to see clearly about one-third of them. Artists likely painted these works between 1353 and 1368, soon after the Black Death devastated the continent.[19] Provence, among the first regions to suffer from the pandemic when it appeared there in 1348, was not alone. Plague swept through much of France, especially from 1360 to 1362.[20]

Many panels feature iconography common across the continent in the late Middle Ages. About one-third of the surviving images show biblical scenes and saints. Another third presents scenes from daily life of clerics and laypeople in medieval Provence. Three tonsured monks stand side by side in one panel, dressed in seemingly identical flowing white robes. Saint Barthelmy holds the knife that brought his martyrdom in Armenia. Saint John is here too, holding a book, and an angel, poised on the verge of flight, looks on. One painting depicts the celebration of mass. Others feature individual men and women, possibly portraits of the donors whose funds made the project possible. Angels can still be seen, their wings crammed to fit into the borders of panels.[21]

Yet many images in Fréjus have no obvious religious theme. One features an acrobat, groups of dancers appear in several panels, and men hunt, fish, and go falconing in still others. Some pictures depict men at war. In one, two women sit at their toilet preparing themselves to be seen, while a companion holds vials of medicine or cosmetics. One woman, gingerly holding her dress, is gathering plants while another grips her formidable hairdo. One talented man takes a ride on the back of a pig. Painters depicted local animals and birds too, including a hound about to pounce on a boar. The artists seem to have been familiar with books depicting wildlife from well beyond Europe's borders, in Asia and Africa. A whole catalog of exotic beasts roamed above the heads of late medieval congregants.[22]

Mingling among these quotidian scenes are depictions of monsters and prodigies. It is one thing for a symbolic lamb to strut around carrying a cross, a well-known visual representation of Christ. But many of the nonhumans do not fit such religious iconography. A painting of a unicorn might not seem too shocking on its own. But what to make of the head of a bald man perched on a

FIGURE 3. The images at Fréjus included the everyday and the exotic—tonsured monks (see the upper left panel), perhaps depictions of some of the brothers who inhabited the church, can be found near exotic animals whose normal territory lay far from the south of France. Portraits likely depict the church's patrons, an acrobat, and nuns in full habit. These pictures of everyday figures are now side by side with depictions of mermaids, blemmye, centaurs, and all manner of human/creature hybrids. Photo by the author. (See Plate 2.)

neck so long that it doubles back in the painting to peer over the creature's nonhuman body? There are centaurs here too, of both sexes, and dragons with jagged teeth. Hybrids abound, with humorous and hideous appendages, while others seem to be crosses of real with mythical beasts. One has a human head on its chest—a blemmye—and, as if that was not terrifying enough, it wields a spear. There are people with the heads of dogs, a popular trope in medieval

FIGURE 4. The images at Fréjus have no obvious order. Depictions of monsters are mounted adjacent to quotidian scenes. Although some of the images in the cloister seem to have few if any known analogs elsewhere, most were local variants of creatures that had long inhabited Europeans' churches, books, and imaginations. Photo by the author.

Europe. Others are unfathomable, such as a creature whose head is a pitcher or another, similarly constructed, whose head resembles a fleur-de-lis.[23]

Scholars have long debated how we should interpret such images in books and on walls. Ever since the dawn of Christendom, particular aspects of its teachings could be expressed succinctly through symbolic language, often involving representations of nature. Three of the four evangelists, for example, were often depicted as animals. St. Mark was a lion and appears as such in one church after another, most famously at Venice's San Marco. But the proliferation of monstrous images in the cloister at Fréjus also constituted part of a larger discussion about the edges of the natural world. Around 1500, learned versions of that discussion no longer took place only in cloisters. By then, printers taking advantage of advances in moveable type produced one book after another about the physical world, facilitating speculation about the nature seen in places like Fréjus and the nature that existed somewhere beyond.

In the past (like now), any individual's understanding of nature came from multiple sources. In the early modern period, on both sides of the Atlantic, authorities on the natural world included parents and other members of the local community, who provided guidance about daily life in a particular place—for example, how to take care of livestock, when to tap a maple tree for syrup, or where to locate fish. Community elders of various kinds shared their wisdom about the world through sermons or oral history. Europeans also had books, which became especially useful for spreading news about the natural world beyond local boundaries, especially if they contained illustrations. To be sure, access to the information in books was of limited utility to someone who could not read, unless a script included pictures. Nonetheless, judging from comments in existing books, some had texts read to them by their literate neighbors. The landscape informed too. Long after Romans left the south of France, to take one example, Christians built churches next to or on top of ancient sacred sites, attempting to draw on the numinous powers that remained. They also recycled spolia, building new churches from the ruins of pagan shrines.[24]

Did early modern Europeans really believe, we might ask ourselves, in the existence of sacred springs at Valles des Nymphes and of the monsters at Fréjus? Could the priests at Fréjus have been try-

FIGURE 5. Located near the town of La Garde-Adhemer in the Rhône-Alpes, Valles des Nymphes features a sacred spring and a Romanesque church, which was first built in the eleventh century. Two hundred years later, the local population moved to a nearby hillside, but the church remained and its supporters eventually added buttresses to prevent it from falling down. The absence of continuing settlement has left the site an ideal vantage point for seeing how locals kept alive knowledge about the spiritual power of one part of a landscape, notably a sacred stream that ran through the woods toward the church (on the opposite side of this picture, with waters presumably filling the pool in the foreground here), despite widespread social and religious change. Photo by the author.

ing to scare the locals into behaving according to church-sanctioned norms by threatening them with the beasts that deviants might encounter in Hell? Could some of the people in that town, perhaps the priests themselves or maybe the church's noble patrons, have heard about the monsters that lurked beyond the edges of Europe? Is it possible that pilgrims who climbed the steep hill to pray at the Basilica of Sainte-Marie-Madeleine in Vézelay in Burgundy to find twelfth-century carvings of the monstrous races in a tableau depicting the Pentecost believed that these creatures had witnessed one of the defining events at the dawn of Christianity?[25]

Europeans had been writing about the monstrous since at least the fourth century before the Common Era. By the eleventh century CE, there was a well-known visual language for depicting monsters, especially the most popular: the dog-headed cynocephali, the one-footed sciapod, the crane-headed man, the two-headed human, and the headless blemmye. One did not need the printing press for such ideas to spread. Medieval *mappae mundi* depicted the monstrous in their margins.[26] The legendary map in Hereford Cathedral included a mandrake with its head upside down as well as depictions of fifty-two other monstrous species.[27] Further, a vibrant tradition of travel literature kept ideas in circulation. Sir John Mandeville's narrative began its epic circulation of the continent in French (probably an Anglo-Norman variant) between 1356 and 1366—in all likelihood, the same years that the painters created one fantastic image after another for the ceiling of the cloister in Fréjus. In the generations that followed, copyists, translators, and painters spread Mandeville's and other fantastic tales across Europe.[28] Did those who read Mandeville or heard about him really believe that somewhere there existed individuals with holes in the middle of their faces for sucking nutrients through reeds? Were there really people with the heads of dogs, or cyclops, or humans with heads on their chest? Some might argue that both storytellers and their audiences recognized such creatures as entertaining nonsense and perhaps condemned Mandeville, if he actually ever existed, for making it all up.

But within a hundred years of its creation, Mandeville's tale spread across the continent, translated and recopied hundreds of times. Christopher Columbus had a copy, as did Leonardo da Vinci.[29] Ralegh, sailing through the Orinoco, told about running into a group similar to blemmyes; he called them "Ewaipanoma" and claimed they were "reported to have their eyes in their shoulders and their mouthes in the middle of their breasts." "Such a nation was written of by Mandevile," he added, "whose reports were holden for fables many yeeres and yet since the East Indies were discovered, we find his relations true of such things as heretofore were held incredible." Ralegh admitted he never saw ewaipanoma with his own eyes, but he was convinced they were real since it was unlikely that so many reporters would conspire to spread falsehoods.[30] One modern editor has identified three hundred surviving manuscript copies of Mandeville's travels, far surpassing similar works such as Marco Polo's, which apparently can be found in seventy manuscripts.[31] The texts would have elicited little shock among Europeans accustomed to viewing the monstrous in their churches. William Shakespeare played on the common knowledge of such figures when Othello tells Desdemona about cannibals and "men whose heads/Do grow beneath their shoulders."[32]

In his first report of the Americas, Columbus wrote to his patrons that he had, as he put it, "not found any monstrous men in these islands, as many had thought"—an indication not of his skepticism about the existence of the monstrous but merely a note that he had just not yet found them as he had expected.[33] Was it his reading of Mandeville that led him to that assertion? The Genoese explorer was on a complicated mission in the 1490s, looking not only for a water route to the Pacific Ocean but also for a place where he might gain access to the realm of the spirits. He searched this world for a possible portal to the Terrestrial Paradise. He believed he found it about one hundred leagues west of the Azores. He could not enter it, though, since he realized that "no one can enter except by God's leave." But he was fairly certain that he had found

FIGURE 6. One did not have to be in a European city to encounter the monstrous. At Serrabone, a lonely priory in the mountains near the border between France and Spain, a series of remarkable carvings reminded the monks of the demonic forces that roamed the world of the spirits. Such carvings, like those in large towns or along well-traveled pilgrimage routes, drew on centuries' old depictions of the creatures that loomed beyond the visible world. Wikimedia Commons.

the location where the elect might be able to cross into a different realm of existence.[34]

In the generations after Columbus, classical wisdom about nature's exotica came to exist side by side with new information arriving in Europe, brought by travelers who had journeyed to parts of the world that their ancestors had never glimpsed. The arrival of this evidence—such as Columbus's surprise at not finding monsters—did not dislodge prevailing European views about the world beyond the continent's edge. The year after Columbus's first report appeared in print, Giulano Dati, a Florence-born poet, who was also a priest, published a version of the explorer's initial report in verse. He made no mention of any monsters, although he did include Columbus's reference to an island populated by cannibals and added details about another peopled by a fierce race of warrior women. But when a new version of his work on Columbus appeared in print in 1494, it included three revealing woodcuts: one depicted giant-footed sciapods and a blemmye, along with well-armed pygmies (similarly not mentioned by Columbus); the second represented a cyclops (labeled a "monoculi"), a hermaphrodite, and a dog-headed man ("canocefali"); and the third had a naked man with gigantic ears, a creature that appears to be half-cow and half-horse, a two-headed snake with one of the heads in human form, a gigantic ant, and three winged creatures, one of them resembling a house cat.[35] The idea of the monster at the margins was, in this case, stronger than the report that indicated that they could not be found there, a legacy of the power of traditional knowledge that was not contained only in ancient manuscripts but also in printed books like the *Nuremburg Chronicle*, which were appearing at nearly the same moment.[36] This may not be surprising since, as the French historian Jacques Le Goff argued over thirty years ago, Europeans could not easily escape their long-held fascination with the Indian Ocean and its denizens—the "Indians" in Columbus's narrative—because they remained in a trance-like state about the East.[37]

Europeans' study of the monstrous constituted a small part of a continent-wide obsession with marvels and wonders.[38] Travelers' tales like Mandeville's circulated widely because they often offered entertaining details about peoples whose actions and appearance

FIGURE 7. Soon after Columbus returned to Europe, his report about what he saw in the Western Hemisphere began to circulate in print, a medium that was then beginning to have a wide impact on how Europeans learned about the world. The Florentine poet and priest Giulano Dati rendered Columbus's narrative into verse, which appeared with this print of the monstrous races included in it. Alamy.com.

differed so markedly from the familiar. But there was a dark side to Europeans' interest in wonders, notably the obsession with malefic, often invisible forces that plagued their communities and could be manipulated, some believed, with magic and staved off with prayer. As the historian Stuart Clark shrewdly observed through close reading of hundreds of early modern texts, Europeans thought *with* demons, many of them in monstrous form.[39]

Nonetheless, discussions of the monstrous reached beyond the constructs of Christian doctrine and interpretation. In 1573, the French anatomist Ambroise Paré published a scientific study of monsters and prodigies. Paré by then had long experience as a surgeon and had been admitted to the confraternity of the Royal College of Surgeons in Paris in 1554. He later became chief surgeon to King Charles IX. While he would eventually run afoul of the capital's physicians, who thought he lacked the proper education to publish his collected writings (which he first did in 1575), his tetralogical work aroused no great animus.[40]

Paré approached his subject as a scientist, not a theologian. "Monsters are things that appear outside the course of Nature (and are usually signs of some forthcoming misfortune)," he wrote, "such as a child who is born with one arm, another who will have two heads, and additional members over and above the ordinary." "Marvels are things," he continued, "which happen that are completely against Nature as when a woman will give birth to a serpent, or to a dog, or some other thing that is totally against Nature." He assured his readers that he had drawn from prevailing authorities, including Pliny, Galen, Aristotle, Lycosthenes, and his contemporary Pierre Boaistuau's *Histoires Prodigieuses*. But he also included recent reports of the monstrous, such as the category of people he referred to as the "maimed," which included girls with impenetrable hymens and people "having spots or warts or wens, or any other thing that is against Nature." Paré offered thirteen "causes of monsters," which included divine intervention; too much, too little, or otherwise corrupted semen during the procreative process; problems in the womb; what he called "the imagination"; and malevolent actions by "wicked spital beggars" or demonic forces. Imagination, as it turns out, could be devilish indeed, as European philosophers and theologians had known since the ninth century. Paré reported the births of children with fur, the four feet of an ox, and the face of a frog. Circumstances other than imagination produced hermaphrodites, stones, or live serpents, which escaped some men's bodies when they peed.[41]

Paré analyzed the creation of some creatures found, among other places, in the paintings at Fréjus (although he did not mention the church). "There are monsters that are born with a form that is half-animal and the other [half] human, or retaining everything [about them] from animals, which are produced by sodomists and atheists who 'join together' and break out of their bounds—unnaturally—with animals," he declared, "and from this are born several hideous monsters that bring great shame to those who look at them or speak of them." Sex with an animal, in this scheme, produced unnatural creatures that "are born half-men and half-animals."[42] Here Paré's writings reflected an elaboration of those of the late medieval French philosopher Nicole Oresme, who tended to discount the role of imagination in the creation of the monstrous and instead sought natural explanations—for example, "that for the most part monsters arise by reason of a deficiency and that there are in them the dispositions of the species which they follow in [the order of] generation, although at times they are mixed with each other."[43]

Paré was one of many sixteenth-century scholars wrestling with the range of creatures found walking or crawling across the Earth. Columbus probably first learned about monsters—and the likelihood they would be present in distant locales—from the French theologian and cosmographer Pierre d'Ailly, whose *Imago Mundi* of 1410 provided ample claims of their existence.[44] But the writings of multiple authorities spread at the time. The works of the ancient historian Julius Solinus circulated across sixteenth-century Europe, telling tales about people with backward feet, each with eight toes, and those he called "monoscelans," also known as sciapods, who could run fast even though they had only a single large foot.[45] Sebastian Münster, creator of a widely reprinted cosmography of the mid-sixteenth century, inserted various images of the monstrous in his pages, including a two-page diagram of *monstra marina* in his widely reprinted *Cosmographia Universallis*, which first appeared in print in the early 1550s. The French physician and natural historian Guillaume Rondolet produced a comprehensive catalog of every known marine species, which included descriptions of fish from the Indies adjacent to sections on the monster Leonin and monstrous fish ("*monstre marin*") in the shape of both a monk in a habit and another resembling a bishop.[46] The French royal cartographer André Thevet, fresh from a relatively brief journey to the Western Hemisphere, included monsters in his *Cosmographie Universelle* in the 1570s.[47] Scholars, echoing the drawings at the edges of medieval maps like that at Hereford, circulated visual evidence of monsters roaming distant places. Among the most prominent was the Swedish cleric Olaus Magnus, who depicted monsters on his massive *Carta Marina* of 1539, a work so large it had to be printed in multiple sheets because no press could handle its size.[48] The Flemish mapmaker Abraham Ortelius's map of Iceland depicted the North Atlantic as chockfull of monsters, many of them capable of destroying a European vessel. Few Europeans had firsthand experience of terrestrial or marine monsters, but many of the learned across the continent had no doubt that they existed.[49]

Consider, as another example, the work of the English naturalist Edward Topsell. Topsell is best known today as the compiler of two major works: *The Historie of Beastes*, published in London in 1607, and *The Historie of Serpents*, published there the following year. In one sense, these books represented Topsell's efforts to complete the catalog of nature begun a half-century earlier by the Swiss polymath Conrad Gesner. Topsell's printed books had long sections on particular animals, including lengthy descriptions of such mundane creatures as horses, pigs, and beavers. But interspersed in his books on beasts he included chapters on monsters, including the sphinx, satyr, winged dragon, and unicorn. Those chapters revealed Topsell's

FIGURE 8. Many sixteenth-century European maps of the oceans depicted sea monsters. While some of the creatures seem far-fetched and were perhaps the product of overactive cartographic imagination rather than actual sightings in the water, mapmakers nonetheless depicted creatures that many believed were real. They might have been right about some of these monsters. Modern marine biologists describe creatures, like the oarfish, which bear an uncanny resemblance to the terrifying swimmers on maps produced by leading cartographers such as the unknown illustrators of the German cosmographer Sebastian Münster's dense volumes describing the world known to Europeans. On the back of this two-page illustration, a reader could find text describing each creature swimming in these seas. Wikimedia Commons.

deep knowledge of European writing on *naturalia*, as well as his desire to be read as an up-to-date scientific observer, which explains his inclusion of the American succarath (or su). [50]

There should be no doubt that Topsell was aware of the newest discoveries in the catalog of nature. He entitled his last book, which was never published, "The Fowles of Heaven," which (judging from clues in the dedication) he likely wrote in 1613 or 1614. The manuscript, now in the collection at the Huntington Library, contains a series of small paintings of birds. Organized alphabetically, the volume includes only birds with species names beginning from A to C. Topsell never explained why he did not finish the work, although he

FIGURE 9. The English naturalist Edward Topsell saw himself as the intellectual and artistic heir to the Swiss scholar Conrad Gesner, who in the middle of the sixteenth century had produced a massive catalog of what he took to be the beasts roaming the earth, both domesticated and wild. In addition to bringing this material to an English-reading public, Topsell also added descriptions and images of some of the creatures Europeans had found in the Americas, including the succarath. But he did not segregate these images from others. Long chapters on livestock could be found adjoining sections on animals only then beginning to penetrate European consciousness. Both of the images here are from Topsell's study of beasts. John Carter Brown Library and Wikimedia Commons.

admitted to his patron, Lord Elsemere, that it had been a struggle to get as far as he did because he suffered from both a paralyzed right arm and the economic burden of having published his books on beasts and serpents. Printers, he confided to Elsemere, "are the men which are rich by making schollers poore"—an idea still held, it might be said, by many modern scholars.[51]

Topsell's manuscript on birds resembles his finished books, with an illustration of each species and then details about its size, behavior, and history. He did not pretend to have studied each bird, but using a common intellectual strategy, his descriptions gained authority through his ability to cite relevant stories or other scholars who had presumably undertaken close examinations of specific species. So, Topsell tells his readers, the Alcatrax, the first bird in the collection, was known to "eminent persons," including King Henry IV of France, who spoke to the Earl of Salisbury, Queen Elizabeth's ambassador to France, about it. He provided a specific reference to Ramusio's *Navigationi et Viaggi*, a book that shaped Elizabethan thinking on the world beyond Europe's borders.[52] He also noted that the Duke of Florence gave a dead "blackmake" to the Bolognese naturalist Ulisse Aldrovandi, who amassed a prodigious collection of both books and specimens before his death in 1605 and whose work was vital for Topsell's.[53]

While virtually all of the birds in the manuscript could be found in Europe and were known (judging from Topsell's citations) by earlier scholars, he also included birds found in Virginia. Topsell, who likely never sailed across the Atlantic, was part of the network of scholars eager to learn more about American nature, in this case from a place claimed by the English and promoted by those eager to establish a presence for the realm on American shores—including the younger Richard Hakluyt, who supplied Topsell with a picture of a Virginia towhee.[54] For the Aushouetta (the thrasher [?]), Aupseo (bluebird), and Aiussaco (flicker), he had pictures only, which he included "without descriptions." The Artamokes (blue jay) fared better: it merited a paragraph explaining that the English in Virginia refused to eat it because its diet of flying spiders and oakworms made it taste poor. But the creature had extraordinary verbal range, able to emulate crows, roosters, turtledoves, and peacocks—a talent that led the Americans to call it "a Linguist."[55] Other Virginia birds also got short shrift; the texts for the Chuguareo (red-winged blackbird), Chuwheeo (towhee), Chungent (modern species unidentified), and Chowankus (female towhee [?]) are all brief, no doubt because European knowledge of these birds was recent and limited. Topsell also included a dual portrait of a bat with two of her young, a sign that the modern division between bats and birds had not yet developed.[56] In addition, Topsell included several pictures of monstrous birds in his chapter on "cocks." There's a picture of a cock with three feet and another with five and hens with more than two feet as well. His text may be the most extensive history of roosters written in early modern Europe, a monument of avian erudition that recalled the long chapters on horses and pigs in his *Historie of Beastes*.[57]

Although Topsell lived until 1625, he apparently never wrote about nature after abandoning the birds. But his works bring us into the early modern pan-Atlantic discussion of nature, particularly to questions about creatures that we now deem fantastic or imaginary. Topsell read Ramusio. So did the younger Richard Hakluyt, who arranged to have narratives written by the French explorer Jacques Cartier, originally printed by Ramusio, translated into English and published in 1580.[58] Hakluyt and Ralegh both read and cited Mandeville. Paré read and cited the French royal cosmographer André Thevet, who shared ideas and manuscripts with Hakluyt when the English scholar lived in Paris in the mid-1580s, not long after Thevet had produced his massive *Cosmographie Universelle*, which included material about the Americas—including a remarkable short chapter about the Island of Rats where he claimed unfortunate shipwreck victims died from eating poisonous rodents the size of rabbits.[59] Hakluyt published Mandeville's account in 1589, and a decade later—when he omitted Mandeville's text from his revised collection of travel narratives, perhaps because it seemed too incredible—he published Ralegh's account of going up the Orinico, in which Ralegh recounted interviews with locals who told him about blemmyes and Amazons, among other monsters. Soon after, a Flemish publisher named Levinus Hulsius published an extract from Ralegh, which included depictions of these monsters. The cycle of citations spiraled ever backward. Every scholar, it seems, knew about the work of Münster and Gesner, two authorities on every living species, including monsters, and references to Pliny appeared with regularity.[60]

European thinking about monsters in the sixteenth century co-existed with observers' accounts of nature entering scientific consciousness as a result of ships crossing the Atlantic. Observers drew no sharp boundaries. As the historians of science Lorraine Daston and Katherine Park have argued, trying to explain the existence of the monstrous—Paré's main goal in his study—was part of scientific inquiry.[61] The American succarath described by Topsell and the blemmyes of the Orinoco reported by Ralegh coexisted with the chowankus and the armadillo, just like the sphinx and dragon could be found in Topsell's catalog alongside the pig and the horse.

Europeans did not need the printing press to carry on discussions about the increasing diversity of nature, but books helped circulate ideas farther and faster. Many of the books rolling off presses in sixteenth- and early seventeenth-century Europe wrestled with questions about nature and human efforts to manipulate it. Agricultural reformers, for example, articulated theories about imposing new order on fields, thereby (so the theory went) expanding crop yields.[62] But older belief systems did not melt away. When Olaus Magnus wrote his history of northern peoples in the middle of the sixteenth century, he reported that the Finns had devised ways to control the winds, employing an ancient practice designed to propitiate the forces of nature.[63] Venetians, dependent on the rich estuaries of the Adriatic, symbolically married the sea every year in an effort to prevent devastating storms.[64] And Europeans continued to believe that monsters existed, close at home and far away—some caused by demonic forces, others by unconventional and threatening actions of women, and still others because they were members of monstrous races.[65] The boundaries between the everyday and the supernatural were porous for many learned Europeans—a belief, as it turned out, that they shared with Americans.

Like Europeans, Americans mastered ways of transmitting information about the world, although they did so via such devices as calendar sticks, quipu, sand paintings, carved glyphs, and, quite likely the most common of all, oral history. Even without printed books or schools, they had educational systems through which they transmitted their cultures and values from one generation to another.[66] It can be difficult to re-create how specific information flowed through some channels, but in the sixteenth century there were Europeans who understood that Americans preserved and shared abundant stores of knowledge. No one today can read quipu, but Europeans knew that it could be read to provide details about the culture and history of people in the Andes.[67]

Indigenous Americans, as Ralegh and Topsell realized, had their own monsters and demons. To be fair, discussion about them tended to be overshadowed in European travel accounts by efforts to describe the riches to be harvested in the Western Hemisphere or the religious and cultural practices of Natives that might make conquest and colo-

FIGURE 10. Given the European interest in monsters, it was hardly surprising that a Flemish printer's edition of Sir Walter Ralegh's narrative of his
journey to the Orinoco included monstrous beings—here a blemmye and an
Amazon—found across the Atlantic Ocean. John Carter Brown Library.

nization difficult. But the monsters were indeed there, as printed books revealed. One edition of Jean de Léry's narrative of his journey to Brazil showed a demon beating Americans.[68] One of Ralegh's printers included depictions of various monsters as well as American creatures previously unknown to Europeans, including the sloth, in a late sixteenth-century edition of his travels to Guiana.[69]

But while Europeans tried to understand monsters and demons in their own communities and to identify any roaming the New World, Americans were not obviously concerned with how a monstrous entity came to be, or at least there is relatively little in the documents from the sixteenth century that suggest a pressing concern. But sources from that period, as well as various oral histories and archaeological remains, do reveal Americans' desire to understand the world beyond daily existence. For many, this meant exploring the relations between the world of humans and the not-human world of the deities, some of them monstrous.

Spirits, a vast number of indigenous Americans understood, were everywhere, and humans needed to appease them in order to survive. Mayans in the Yucatan created openings to buildings that resembled a fierce animal's jaws, known to archaeologists as serpent-column portals. The fang-like stones hanging over an opening symbolized, as one twentieth-century observer wrote, the "descent of the celestial monster into the interior of the temple, bringing with it benefits from the beyond."[70] Columns depicted Tlahuizcalpante-cuhtli or the "jaguar-serpent-bird," a creature capable of tearing out a person's internal organs.[71] Animals, insects, and birds played prominent roles in American origins tales.[72] Disparate groups of Algonquian speakers in the American Northeast believed that the origins of the world lay in the actions of a hare, a moose, or a bear. "For native North Americans," the religion scholar Catherine Albanese has observed, "the numinous world of nature beings was always very close, and the land itself expressed their presence." Such spirits could

take human form as well and leave a permanent mark on the landscape, as Americans across the continent realized. The Kiowas, who
had come into the world through a hollow log, explained the unique
shape of Devil's Tower in the Black Hills as the result of a boy who
had become a bear chasing his seven sisters up a tree: they escaped
into the sky and became the Big Dipper and the tree became the
mountain, its deeply scarred walls the result of the bear clawing his
way upward during the pursuit. From that moment on, the Kiowa
novelist N. Scott Momaday has written, "The Kiowas have kinsmen
in the night sky." The event changed the course of their history.
"However tenuous their well-being, however much they had suffered and would suffer again," Momaday added, "they had found a
way out of the wilderness." These Kiowa migrations, across the
plains toward the Rainy Mountain and in the spiritual transit of the
sisters, were examples of Americans' understanding of the relationship between the everyday world and the world of the spirits. The
boundaries between these spheres were as porous for many Americans as they were for many Europeans. As the art historian Diana
Magaloni Kerpel has noted, the Nahuas "lived in a universe in which
the stars, water, mountains, and some objects were regarded as beings that were as animated and alive as animals and people."[73]

Humans and animals could change shape, in real life and in the
realm of dreams. Mandan cosmology tells of a woman bearing nine
male puppies after having sex with a dog. They then lived together at
Dog Bear Butte, a locale populated by spirits.[74] A Wyandot infor-
mant named B. N. O. Walker reported in November 1911 that there
had once been seven stars in the Pleiades, the heavenly bodies of
seven sisters. But a young Wyandot man fell in love with the one he
found the fairest, and she eventually agreed to return to Earth regu-
larly to be his wife. "This is why, nowadays, we can see among the
Pleiades only six of the maiden sisters," Walker reported. "Sometimes the shadow of the seventh one may just be perceived."[75] The

Pleiades were no ordinary constellation for the indigenous peoples of northeastern North America, who knew that when these stars reached a certain point in the sky, the last threat of freezing had passed and it was the time to plant their corn.[76]

The idea that spiritual forces shaped landscapes could be found across North America. "The material world was a holy place," Albanese noted, "and so harmony with nature beings and natural forms was the controlling ethic, reciprocity the recognized mode of interaction." Native peoples of western Massachusetts believed that an enormous beaver once prevented locals from getting fish they wanted. According to one legend, recorded by the antiquarian Deacon Phineas Field in 1871 (and subsequently published in 1890), the Americans held a powwow to summon the feared and powerful monster named Hobmock (or Hobomok, not to be confused with the Wampanoag named Hobbamok who provided assistance to the English Pilgrims who had come ashore in Plymouth in 1620). Hobmuck appeared and, so Field reported, "waded the river until he found the beaver, and so hotly chased him that he sought to escape by digging into the ground." But Hobmuck guessed the beaver's scheme and, according to another nineteenth-century local historian, used the trunk of a vast oak tree to dispatch the beaver with a massive blow across his neck. The beaver sank into the pond "and turned to stone." The head became modern-day South Sugarloaf Mountain, the body formed North Sugarloaf, and the tail can be seen in the ridge of the Pocumtuck Range. In *The Maine Woods*, the naturalist Henry David Thoreau reported that a Penobscot named Joseph Polis had told him in 1858 that a mountain around Penobscot Bay had once been a cow moose, as its shape revealed.[77]

Indigenous oral history explains the formation of landscapes across North America. Mandan cosmogony tells how the Lone Man and the First Creator partnered to make the Mississippi Valley, with the former establishing lakes and grasslands while the latter created

FIGURE 11. The Pocumtuck Range in modern western Massachusetts, with the body of the beaver to the right and the head in the center. Photo: Ish Ishwar, Wikimedia Commons.

bison and hills. They met up at the confluence of the Missouri and Heart Rivers, the "center of the world" as First Creator described it, and only then peopled the lands with humans.[78] In the southeast of the North American continent, Yuchi, Creek, and Cherokee origins tales note that a great buzzard-shaped ridge in their landscapes. One Choctaw myth attributed the sound of thunder to a buzzard laying eggs in the clouds. In this regional folklore, as the anthropologist Shepard Krech III has noted, "the boundaries between birds, men, and other beings are amorphous and easily transgressed."[79]

The idea that spiritual forces shaped landscapes can be found in many indigenous American communities, including those that had extensive contact with Europeans in the sixteenth century. A Malecite named Jim Paul from St. Mary, New Brunswick, told an anthropologist in the early 1910s about various locales that had been produced by the god Gluscap. Once, so Paul related, Gluscap had gone hunting for beavers. But when he reached Mactiquack Creek, he could not move easily with his snowshoes, so he took them off. "To-day you can see them," Paul reported, "for those two islands opposite Mactiquack are called 'Gluscap's Snowshoes.'" Then he traveled "to the mouth of the Kennebecasis, where the beavers had their homes." He destroyed one large lodge, allowing water to carry the physical remains downstream, where they formed an island the Malecites called Kikw Mikhigin for "the sod which broke away." Soon he encountered other beaver and drove them out of their lodge, which became known as Long Island, also in Kennebacasis Bay (in modern New Brunswick). With his trusty dog by his side, he hunted yet other beaver and killed them. "Even to this day," Paul reported, "you can see the red spots on the white granite where their blood dripped."[80] Some Hurons told the Recollect brother Gabriel Sagard that a distinctive rock formation along a river about 150 leagues from Québec had once been a man and the stones took the shape of his outstretched arms. Whenever they passed in a canoe, so Sagard reported about his journey of 1623–1624, they threw tobacco "into the water against the rock itself" and "say to it, 'Here, take courage, and let us have a good journey,' together with some other speech that I did not understand."[81]

The Jesuit missionary Paul Le Jeune, who had first arrived in Canada in 1632, learned how humans, animals, and monsters coexisted in one Algonquian vision of the past. He wrote about a deity the locals called Messou, who had gone out hunting with a group of lynx (rather than dogs), who were also his brothers. The lynx chased an elk into the middle of a lake but then disappeared under the surface. When Messou arrived, a bird told him that "certain animals or monsters" had grabbed his companions and held them under water. Messou leapt in to rescue them, which caused the lake to overflow and flood the world. Messou then realized he would need to rebuild the land. To do so, he first sent a raven and then an otter to find some soil; both failed. Messou then commanded a muskrat, which succeeded. "With this bit of earth," Le Jeune reported, "he [Messou] restored everything to its condition." He transformed himself "into a thousand kinds of animals" to exact revenge against the monster. And then, Le Jeune wrote, Messou, "this great Restorer, having married a muskrat, had children who repeopled the world." Le Jeune told the story to reveal, as other European visitors had discovered, that Americans often had religious beliefs that included descriptions of ancient events, such as the creation of the world or the biblical flood. "I confess that the Savages have no public or common prayer, nor any form of worship usually rendered to one who they hold as God, and their knowledge is only as darkness," Le Jeune acknowledged. "But it cannot be denied that they recognize some nature superior to the nature of man."[82]

Because the gods did not exist in a distant past and then disappear, Americans in one community after another found ways to maintain active ties to them, typically in a sequence of rituals marking the most important moments of the year.[83] The Iroquois, among others, inhabited a landscape crowded with spirits. As the historian Daniel Richter has written, "Other-than-human persons as game animals, trees, or the wind possessed spiritual power that could be turned to human advantage or human destruction." In such a world, properly propitiated deities would allow an animal to be hunted and a lake to be crossed. But without the correct rituals, doom threatened. "If humans neglected their reciprocal obligations and offended these beings," Richter continued, "the results could be hunger, sickness, injury, or death."[84] Such practices could devastate a human body, at least temporarily. The Creeks ingested a purgative known as the black drink, a locally produced caffeine-rich liquid. They knew they would become ill, but through their vomiting, they would also be ritually cleansed, an act of purification that pleased the deities who controlled the success of annual crops.[85] For their part, the Hurons tried to appease Aataentsic, the female spirit who created humanity but who was, as one anthropologist put it, "an evil nature" who "spent much of her time trying to undo" the good works of her son Iouskeha. Tawiscaron, Iouskeha's brother, unfortunately took after his mother, or at least until Iouskeha drubbed him in a fight and he fled. Thereafter, mother and son lived together in a wooden house, the one doing all she could to hurt people and the other trying his best to aid them. Humans did all they could to please the son.[86]

Cultural practices differed across the Americas, of course, but similarities existed from one place to another. One community after another across the hemisphere believed that tobacco had sacred powers. It was present at the creation, as suggested by the primordial man and woman wearing sacred tobacco gourds in the *Codex Borbonicus*, an early sixteenth-century Aztec manuscript.[87] Everywhere indigenous Americans linked tobacco to religious practice, quite possibly because ingesting it could produce psychotropic effects, including hallucinations, that suggested users had access to forces beyond the visible world.[88] As the historian Christopher Parsons has remarked for Natives around the Great Lakes region, "Tobacco was a gift to human beings to facilitate their relationships with beings with powers upon which they depended."[89] Mi'kmaq (Micmac) legend reveals that when the culture hero Gluscap wanted to travel across a large body of water, he summoned a whale, who agreed to carry him on the condition that Gluscap share a pipe filled with tobacco with him.[90] The French traveler Nicolas Perrot witnessed Algonquian hunters propping up the body of a just-killed bear and puffing into its mouth and then pushing the smoke out of its nose, an effort to share the sacred power of the plant with the spirits that controlled the animals.[91] Europeans were eager to harness what they believed were the beneficial aspects of tobacco, but they feared its usage in indigenous American rituals and needed to find a way to control it. Like Americans, early European observers did not doubt the potential religious power of the plant or its ability to allow those who consumed it to communicate with otherworldly spirits.[92]

What Perrot witnessed in the eighteenth century was a cultural practice that likely dated back to the origins of hunting among Americans. Everyone knew that success at the hunt required finding game. Some animals, notably deer, could often be found in large numbers on the margins of native settlements, drawn to what biologists refer to as "edge" environments, primarily the tall grasses that sprouted in the zones between forests and fields.[93] But other animals were more elusive. Other than beaver, which could be found by locating a pond with a lodge in the middle, animals roamed over large distances. To find them meant learning their habits and figuring out where they would be in any given season. Some Americans manipulated the environment, notably by using fire to hem in animals and direct them toward the killing zone, a technique that worked for animals ranging from rabbits to bison.[94] They also prayed to the deities that controlled the movements of animals. If their supplications worked—if the gods took their prayers and actions as a sign of respect—then the deities would tell hunters where to obtain game. And so the peoples who hunted buffalo—Mandan, Blackfeet, and Blood, among others—created rituals to appease the gods, using tobacco, sacred stones, and medicine bundles in rituals of propitiation. Failure in the hunt signified a failure of humans—not as hunters but as people who had not done enough to please the forces that controlled the movement of buffalo across the grasslands.[95]

But harvesting quarry was not the end of a hunt since Americans needed to propitiate the gods with other rituals. Peoples on the plains understood that they needed to consume every part of a bison's body—horns, fur, skin, tongue, organs, hooves, blood, and brains. That cultural imperative combined with the utility of the bison's remains encouraged Americans to harvest each part of the corpse efficiently.[96] Across sub-Arctic Canada, hunters who took too

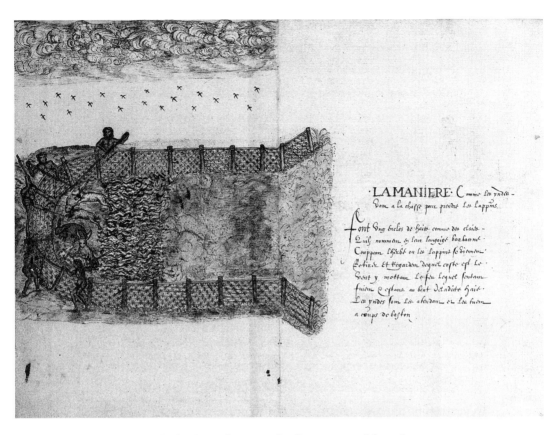

·LAMANIERE· C omme les yndie·
Bom a la chaffe pour prendre les Lappins.

font Sng bicles de haie comme des clois·
Quilz nomment en leur langaige bazlacane·
Couppam Chicbi ou les Lappins se dresent·
Pohier et regardent dequel coste est Le·
Sent y mettant Le fue Lequel sontam
fuient & estoua au hent Ditadicte haie·
Les yndes som les afentans et les fuien
a coups de bafton.

FIGURE 12. By the sixteenth century, few Europeans used fire to hunt game, so the rarity of such a scene may have convinced an unknown European illustrator to include this image of a rabbit hunt from the Caribbean. The technique depicted here, and described in the accompanying text, was likely not practiced, and was possibly unknown, in sixteenth-century Europe, where fears of potential wood shortages would have discouraged such techniques. Courtesy of the Morgan Library.

many animals or failed to please the spirits of the animals, the so-called keepers of the game, failed because the deities had the ability to prevent humans from finding their quarry. Since these nonhuman spirits also determined whether humans became ill, the relationship between hunters and their prey took on significance beyond finding sufficient food to live in areas where agriculture could not sustain human communities.[97] To the present day, the Mistassini Cree fear offending Ciiwetinsuu, "the spirit of the North Wind," which lurks across the winter landscape; any hunter who left any blood on the snow risked its wrath. Elaborate rules dictated how hunting parties needed to treat each part of their prey, all intended to prevent spiritual affronts.[98] Inuit fashioned fishhooks from whale bones, harpoon weights from walrus tusks, and arrowheads from caribou bones, a practice possibly intended to align material and spiritual practices.[99] Performed with the proper reverence, the four-day Mandan ceremony of Okipa lured bison closer and made for a successful quarry.[100]

Americans' use of animals and their remains often startled European observers, perhaps because most of the visitors came from societies that had abandoned hunting animals as a principal source for obtaining protein. Instead, Europeans relied on domesticated livestock, primarily sheep, swine, and cattle. While living in close proximity to these ungulates could cause medical problems, notably by providing fertile grounds for the development of viruses that moved between species, the advantages of a ready supply of meat outweighed the disadvantages of living near large beasts. City dwellers also reduced their contact with offal by limiting the districts of urban areas where butchers tossed animal carcasses.[101]

Americans, by contrast, did not domesticate animals for their meat, though some kept dogs and Andean peoples relied on the labor and wool of llamas and alpacas. Unlike Europeans, indigenous Americans did not fence in these animals but instead let them roam free. According to the Spanish naturalist José de Acosta, who traveled through Peru in the 1570s, there was no need to "spend money on shoeing them, or for saddles or saddlebags, or for feeding them barley; rather, they serve their masters for nothing, being satisfied with the grass that grows in the countryside."[102] Some Americans also kept fowl. The Huguenot traveler Jean de Léry reported that the Tupinambás of Brazil had ducks, but they would not eat a species they labeled the *upec* because, Léry wrote, they believed that "if they were to eat of an animal like this that walks so heavily, it would keep them from running when they are being pursued by their enemies."[103] While some indigenous American communities integrated Old World livestock into their economies, some remained suspicious of Europeans' and Euro-American colonists' close relationship with ungulates long after the period of initial contact.[104]

The need to respect the spirits imposed certain restrictions on Americans. They were not always conservationists, as suggested by a popular stereotype of modern indigenous cultures.[105] But since some, and perhaps many, Americans understood that they needed good relations with the deities so they would be successful on the hunt, and with their plants, and fishing, or even for survival, it made sense not to offend the spirits. The Beothuks, who inhabited modern Newfoundland, feared a monster that came from the sea to punish those who had not behaved properly.[106] Even to the present day, the Runa of the Amazon fear the arrival of *runa puma*, a Quichuan phrase for a human-jaguar, which might devour the unwary.[107] Some Quichua-speaking peoples of modern-day Ecuador still learn to sleep face up to prevent a jaguar attack since the beast will turn away from someone staring at it. That modern belief represents consistency; the ancestors of these people claimed in the late sixteenth century that a spirit in the form of a cow ("*en forma del vaca*") told them they should rebel against Spanish colonists.[108] Inuit would not eat seal or walrus out of season to avoid offending the deities that protected those at sea in kayaks.[109] Salteaux and Mistassini Cree stripped the bark off trees, painted them, and hung bones on the limbs of these *mistikuan* or "made trees." Montagnais/Naskapi practice demanded that a hunter use dreams to try to communicate with the spirit of the caribou and kept some bones from bears to harvest their spiritual power.[110]

Differing cultures of nature—European on one hand and American on the other—dictated human success in particular environments. So, while the model of the Columbian Exchange suggests that Europeans should have universally prevailed, the situation was not so clear across the hemisphere, especially in the Arctic lands of modern-day Nunavut, which was and remains inhabited by Inuit. Europeans who ventured into the area in the sixteenth century (and long after) believed this was one of the most inhospitable places on earth and thus reasoned that civilization could not exist there. Many of them who saw Inuit believed that the locals were savages incapable of such basic human tasks as cooking. Relying on an ancient European conceit, these visitors claimed that Inuit were cannibals ready to murder and consume any outsider who came along.[111]

It is true that the Arctic can be a dangerous place, even in our age of global warming. Europeans knew well that polar bears killed and ate people, and snowdrifts in some places could be, according to early modern observers, thirty feet high. Bitter winds could freeze human skin and eyes. Newcomers to the area who had not learned to eat the fast-growing spring grasses could suffer from scurvy, which hollowed out their faces and made their teeth fall out. Try as they might, Europeans could not find a way to live there in the sixteenth century, even though they recognized the advantages of establishing permanent settlements to support explorers seeking the Northwest Passage.[112]

This was a difficult place to live but not impossible. Survival, as the Inuit understood, came from making a bargain with the gods. Appease the sea goddess Sedna, they knew, and she would bring the seals close to the surface or on to the shore so that hunters could kill them. Use the proper equipment for killing an animal—bones from a bird to make an arrow to hunt birds and bones from seals for fishhooks—and the pursuit would be a success. Those who failed to establish positive relations with the gods would die. Inuit knew how

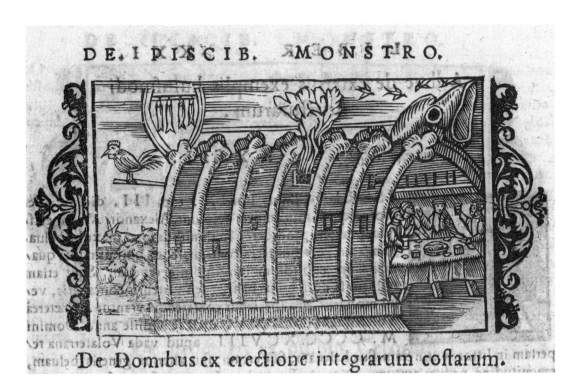

FIGURE 13. Europeans who ventured to the northern reaches of the Western Hemisphere in the sixteenth century tended to stay only a brief time, in part because they did not know how to adapt to a physical environment so foreign to what they knew at home. The Inuit, by contrast, understood how to live in the Arctic because they adapted their economy to the resources that existed there. It might be difficult to harpoon a whale, but whale bones washed ashore with regularity. Erected into a frame, the bones could be covered with the skin of caribou in order to fend off the worst of the winter chill. Europeans already had some notion of the utility of such remains, which the Swedish cleric Olaus Magnus had described in his study of the northern part of the continent in the early sixteenth century. John Carter Brown Library.

to strike the spiritual bargain because they understood that the world of the living and the world of the spirits were intertwined. When a hunter died, according to one prevailing belief, he would reemerge in a parallel place—a sea filled with kayaks bobbing on the waves, successful with every toss of his spear. Inuit understood the cycle of seasons and the importance of the daylight too. Each year they would burn tobacco, which they had to obtain through an indigenous trade network, in a ritual they called "smoking the Sun."[113] If their rituals worked, endless summer days would draw countless numbers of migrating birds whose carcasses could be hung and chilled in stone enclosures, remaining edible through an entire winter.[114] This kind of success only came to those who knew how to read nature's signs, adapt to its demands, and propitiate the gods. In the north, Inuit managed, and Europeans failed.

Before 1492, Europeans and Americans inhabited separate worlds. Within each of these physical arenas, human relationships with nature differed from one locale to another, even within relatively close distances. Peoples of mountainous interiors lived very differently from populations along major rivers. Human communities that relied on agriculture tended to be far larger than those based on hunting or fishing. Residents of wintry climes and those who inhabited balmy coasts lived, worked, and thought differently about their environments. Culture mattered, of course, which explains the vastly different kinds of settlements to be found in similar climates on either side of the ocean.

But wherever they lived, the peoples of the Atlantic basin all understood that the line separating the visible world from the invisible was not always obvious. Venetians married the sea. Algonquians blew smoke into the lifeless body of a bear. Each had the same goal: to please the nonhuman agents that controlled elements of the natural world. When fourteenth-century Christians in Fréjus walked past those monsters on their way to mass, they might have laughed at the fabulous creations above their heads. But European scholars in the sixteenth century tried to explain how, not if, such creatures came into existence. Those once-vibrant panels represented the range of natural and supernatural beings that shared their world—their neighbors, their patrons, their livestock, their clerics, and, yes, also the monsters that roamed not far away. In this way, Europeans were perhaps more similar to Americans at the dawn of the sixteenth century than many would have liked to imagine.

CHAPTER TWO

A New Ecology

The Huntington Library in San Marino, California, possesses a set of maps bound together in an atlas apparently owned by Nicolas Vallard of Dieppe in 1547. Little is known about Vallard. The atlas that now bears his name originally consisted of fifteen individual, hand-painted maps as well as four pages of instructions for how to read a compass at particular latitudes. The maps themselves occupy a curious niche: they are insufficiently detailed to provide real guidance to mariners, who would likely never haul such a lavish book on board their ships, and they are filled with fine paintings better suited for a palace than a captain's berth. The audience was in all likelihood domestic—the kinds of individuals who might fund an expedition to a distant part of the world but would not go there themselves. The plentiful illustrations, glimmering in places with gold leaf, tell two stories: Europeans and the inhabitants of the Mediterranean basin inhabit cities and walk about fully clothed; denizens of the Western Hemisphere and Africa live in territories populated by large animals and seem to have no need for extensive clothing. Among the unclothed were people inhabiting lands to the south of the Straights of Magellan—that is, the fabled Patagonia giants who lived, according to one sheet in the atlas, in an as-yet unseen southern continent, which Europeans believed existed but had not yet discovered.[1] The

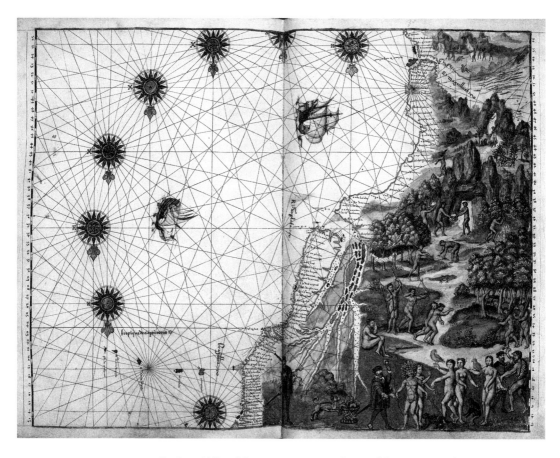

FIGURE 14. By the middle of the 1540s, Europeans knew of the existence of the Straits of Magellan but possessed no evidence about the existence of Antarctica. A continent known as "Terra Incognita Australis" did appear on maps during the century, but it was there to fit a European understanding that all of the parts of the world needed to be in geographical balance, with as much territory north of the equator as to its south. Yet despite the absence of firsthand observation, the creator of this map in the "Vallard Atlas" nonetheless presumed that these extreme southern lands, which are painted on this map south of modern Chile and Argentina, housed giants, occupants who were so far from civilization that they would have walked around naked. In other words, presumptions about culture rather than about environment dictated the visual representation of the unknown continent's not-yet seen inhabitants. Here and throughout, the maps in the "Vallard Atlas" are oriented with south at the top of the page. San Marino, Huntington Library, HM 00029. http://www.digital-scriptorium.org. (See Plate 6.)

book also contains a third, less obvious narrative: a mythological fable, seemingly unrelated to the maps, which unfolds along the borders of the first five sheets, which otherwise depict parts of the Old World and, perhaps, the coasts of Australia.[2]

To sixteenth-century Europeans, clothing was a marker of civilization, so the depiction of people without a stitch on their bodies constituted a major statement. The Americans' nudity also reveals that the "Vallard," like many other European depictions of the Western Hemisphere, was as much a work of imaginative ethnography as it was one of geography. Taken together, these maps are as much about European cultures as they are about what weary travelers would find when they docked their ships in foreign harbors.

The "Vallard Atlas" was bound in 1805 when the maps had come into the possession of Prince de Bénévent Charles Maurice de Talleyrand-Périgord. The maps came together in Dieppe, the port that was the home for cartographers who benefited from the patronage of King Francis I, who ruled from 1515 to 1547. Francis had a keen interest in maps and mapmakers.[3] The atlas pays homage to Francis in an unlikely spot: he can be seen astride a dolphin, apparently in command of the seas south of Africa—an image that would have angered the Portuguese, who by then had become the most powerful Europeans in those waters. Indeed, that same visual device, but featuring Manuel I of Portugal instead of Francis, could be found on the Waldseemüller world map produced in Strasbourg in 1507 and also on Lorenz Fries's *carta marina* of 1530. The Dieppe artists, using a venerable artistic strategy, inserted a powerful patron into the image even if, as in this case, doing so made the map seem less credible to anyone who knew the political situation on the seas.[4]

The cartographers working in Dieppe welcomed news of Atlantic discoveries, which they translated into visual form. Their collective efforts established the city as a locale for expertise about long-distance exploration, which it remained for decades to come. In 1599, when the younger Richard Hakluyt published the narrative of the explorers Richard Rainolds and Thomas Dassel, who traveled to the Senega and Gambra Rivers near Guinea, he noted that sailors from Dieppe had joined Portuguese and Spanish merchants in the local trade in ivory, gold, rice, hides, and wax.[5] The city's reputation as a base for brave navigators was enduring; King Louis XIV in 1668 noted that the port had by then long played a central role in making foreign discoveries.[6]

Cartographers affiliated with the city constituted what is now called the "Dieppe school." By 1570, its members had produced seven manuscript atlases in addition to six world charts, including Jean Rotz's "Boke of Idrography," now in the collection of the British Library, and a related world chart of 1543 by Guillaume Brouscon, a native of Le Conquet, now in the holdings of the Huntington.[7] Unnamed contributors built tables for mariners to measure latitude and techniques for plotting prevailing winds.[8] Although their creators were based in the same town, the details on these maps varied tremendously. The Brouscon world chart, for example, contains very little information about the northern parts of the world and even ignores the alleged Northwest and Northeast Passages that European scholars believed to exist, although the chart provides precise details about southern passages, including the Straits of Magellan (*les zort de magalan*) and the Cape of Good Hope (*cap de bonsouzance*). Brouscon's map also offers few details about territorial interiors, although he did note, as did mapmakers, crucial place names—such as Sagane and Ochleage, likely the Iroquoian settlements of Stadacona and Hochelaga, identified by the Breton explorer Jacques Cartier who had sailed up the St. Lawrence River in the 1530s and early 1540s. Brouscon, like other members of the Dieppe school, also depicted the location of shoals, another sign of the utility of such charts for potential sponsors of expeditions who knew that running aground thousands of miles from home could be the equivalent of a death sentence for both their ships, a major financial investment, and their crews.[9]

These atlases and charts provide a vivid impression of European views about the nature of the Atlantic as well as early impressions of the people and resources of the particular places. Elephants, lions, and camels roam across Rotz's charts of Africa, for example, and a brown or black bear wanders through Labrador in the Canadian Maritimes.[10] Such images might seem fanciful, but these maps conveyed compelling information about natural resources. Rotz, for example, identified the waters off Newfoundland where Europeans fished and guessed—correctly—where buffalo roamed in the North American interior.[11] But such seeming accuracy blended together with fearful nightmares, most notably in Rotz's identification of the "Co[a]st of cannibals" (modern-day Guiana) and elaborate scenes of human carnage in Brazil.[12] Flesh eaters, who appeared in European maps as early as Martin Waldseemüller's *carta marina* produced in Strasbourg in 1516, became the most common trope in sixteenth-century European representations of the region.[13]

More impressive than the Rotz—at least in terms of the quality and variety of its illustrations—is the "Vallard Atlas." The maps here came from the hand of someone—or two people—who had seen Portuguese portolans or sea charts of the Atlantic basin. It is most famous today because it might contain the first European representation of the east coast of Australia.[14] But that geographical curiosity aside, the "Vallard" is well known for the spectacular quality of its maps, which are among the most aesthetically pleasing of any emanating from Europe in the sixteenth century.[15]

Attracted by the quality of the images, we might miss one of the underlying benefits of close analysis of these maps. While they reveal natural resources in situ, such maps also provide clues about the new ecology of the sixteenth-century Atlantic basin. That is, these two-dimensional representations of the place Europeans called the New World depict visual arenas where promoters' hopes met novel perceptions of nature and observations of distant cultures. Lions and turtles coexist easily with native coastal peoples, while multi-hued birds hitch rides on freshly harvested brazilwood trees. There were risks, to be sure; the Tupinambás and other native peoples depicted in the "Vallard" attacked their enemies, as the bleeding head of a European man revealed to any who saw the atlas. But the risks of possible death seemed worthwhile, especially if Europeans could manage to find the labor needed to extract precious goods, either to supplement European provisions or perhaps to replace commodities that had become rare or too expensive, such as dyewood from South or East Asia or beaver pelts from Russia.[16]

The "Vallard Atlas" and other similar cultural productions goaded viewers to travel across the Atlantic. If one could survive a journey where shipwrecks were common, as an entire genre of Portuguese shipwreck narratives informed readers in the sixteenth century,[17] the rewards might be spectacular. By the time cartographers assembled the "Vallard," other images of the natural resources of the Western Hemisphere were already circulating in Europe. Among them was the so-called "Atlas Miller" of 1519, the beautiful creation of the Portuguese painter António de Holanda now housed at the Bibliothèque Nationale in Paris. Holanda depicted Brazilian resources likely based on the narratives of Pedro Álvares Cabral as well as deer, bear, and foxes of Canada presumably drawn from reports of the Corte Real brothers, who had explored the Labrador coast at the turn of the century. This atlas named that northern territory Terra Corte Regalis in their honor.[18]

The "Atlas Miller" represents some of the earliest European knowledge of American nature. There is much less information for Canada than for Brazil, for example, but the details of South American bird life and dyewood trees suggest how the importation of American goods might entice Europeans. Each of the maps of the Western Hemisphere also depicts an abundance of trees across the Western Hemisphere, visual markers that cannot be found in the maps in the same atlas that depict Europe. The contrast points to what would become one of the greatest ecological transformations of the early modern age—the thinning of American forests to satisfy European demands for dyewood (in Brazil), furniture (mahogany in the greater Caribbean basin), housing materials, and fences. Some Europeans were especially eager to harvest naval stores. "There are pynes infinite especially by the Sea-coast and many other sortes," the English traveler William Strachey wrote in the early seventeenth century, "the use of which are Comodious for shipping, Pipe-staues, Clab-bourd, yards, and Mastes for shipping." Ecological change was everywhere a localized phenomenon, but the effects escalated as newcomers, eager to obtain wood products after the centuries-long thinning of their own forests as well as cleared land for agriculture and pasturage from New England to Brazil, gained ever-firmer control over land in the Western Hemisphere.[19]

Europeans who crossed the Atlantic intending to establish colonial settlements did not arrive empty-handed. They loaded livestock on their ships and at times accidentally brought along plants and pathogens. Plant seeds could have been lodged in the hooves of ungulates, for example.[20] Still, animals only boarded ships if captains and their commercial sponsors believed that the benefits of long-distance travel outweighed the many known risks. Transporting a cow might make sense for a group of travelers who wanted milk or meat upon arrival, but they were not easy shipboard companions. Keeping them alive meant bringing along hay by the barrel full, and keeping everyone else on board happy meant constantly cleaning up after the animals. They also needed fresh water for the beasts as well as themselves. (Sailors in the North Atlantic learned to get fresh water from puddles on the tops of icebergs, but most Old World livestock reached the Western Hemisphere on ships that sailed too far south to take advantage of such resources.[21]) And of course cows did not travel alone. Westward-sailing Europeans who planned to stay for a while brought pigs, sheep, and horses too. Even casual visitors brought dogs along, in addition to the cats that invariably stowed away on ships, which were useful hunters of the mice and rats that set up burrows in wooden vessels at port. The creator of the map of Labrador in the "Vallard" included three happy domesticated dogs playing, their identities marked by the red collars around their necks, and another dog, likely of European origin, among a group of travelers in Brazil.[22]

Those who arranged to stock ships in European ports made their investments only after determining that the costs would be worth the returns. They needed two things. First, they wanted information about what they might harvest abroad. Second, they had to have some sense of how to get home again. The lure for merchants was gold, furs, and spices. For Bible-bearing missionaries, the temptation was countless heathen souls, which needed to be harvested for the Christian God. But crucial to the success of all European transatlantic ventures was knowledge about the environment. It meant the difference between fortune and ruin as well as life and death. And it meant as well being sensitive to how circumstances changed, often as a result of an ever-larger number of people and ships crossing the ocean.

Maps bear a complicated relationship to nature. In the early modern era, many maps, such as those in the "Vallard," contained suggestive illustrative material, either in cartouches or on the maps themselves. Yet this information often masked cartographic uncertainty and reflected the representational strategies of the cartographer.[23] If a mapmaker did not have details about a particular place, he or she could fill otherwise empty space with familiar and fanciful decorations. However flawed, their artistic elaboration showed what the mapmaker thought visitors might find in particular locales. Over time, cartographers modified the technique. When they had insufficient details about local geography (for example, the location of mountains or the courses of rivers), they created cartouches to convey what little information they had. The Dutch cartographer Herman Moll, working in the early eighteenth century, created a large map of eastern North America with a sizable cartouche depicting a vast colony of beaver organized in an assembly line of lumber production near Niagara Falls. The details are incorrect. Beaver do not live in large colonies, nor do they stand on their hind legs carrying wood like small furry humans.[24] Despite its inaccurate depiction of this place, the cartouche beckoned observers: go to this region and you will find large populations of beaver, which remained throughout the early modern period the most profitable fur-bearing animal in the Western Hemisphere.[25] The artists who created the "Vallard Atlas" were masters of the form. The map that may possibly depict eastern Australia is nonsensical. Men and women in yellow tunics inhabit a seeming paradise while an apparently more primitive population, possibly naked, battles in the distance. The appeal to the primordial garden can be found in the picture's emotional centerpiece: a tableau of a family, with a man offering an apple to a woman and an infant—an inverted Eden for the upside-down world of the Antipodes.[26]

The maps in the "Vallard" project a confident if uneven understanding of the world beyond Dieppe. Hence, palaces and place names crowd Europe. Italy is so packed that the artist placed a portrait of the pope near Finland, an empty place little known to mapmakers that could be filled with an image of the Holy See. Heraldic symbols substitute for monarchs in Britain—with the Cross of St. George atop England and Ireland and the Cross of St. Andrew demarcating Scotland. European monarchs wear crowns while North African sultans or emirs, who are similarly prominent and seated, sport turbans. All leaders bear scepters, marking their authority in a fashion intelligible to Europeans. Europe and North Africa, the image asserts, need no addi-

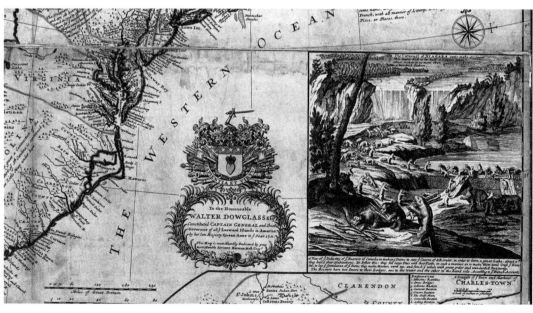

tional exploration. They are understood, familiar, and already well populated, and there are no new resources to harvest there.[27]

By comparison, territory farther from Europe—and not even as far as Australia—presented challenges to the cartographers in Dieppe. The Red Sea appears on one map but with few place names along its shores, which reflected Europeans' less frequent access to the region since the Crusades. Similarly, the fabled Christian king and prince Prester John appears seated on a throne in East Africa, although many Europeans knew him to be a figment of ancient fantasies. But he is located near a grand city surrounded by water, a likely effort to depict the center of Ethiopian civilization on an island in Lake Tana, a place described by medieval European travelers. An African king along the eastern shores of the continent might have been an effort to visualize the story reported by Marco Polo about the sultan of 'Adal, who reigned over Zeila or "Zella," as it is written on the map.[28] By the middle decades of the sixteenth century, many Europeans had learned about exotic animal species found in Africa. So it was no surprise that the artist depicted a map of the continent featuring elephant, rhinoceros, lion, camel, crocodile, and various apes. The artist also added two of the most widely represented monsters, a blemmye and a cynocephalus. The mapmaker drew on the rich European tradition of the monsters beyond the

FIGURES 15 (*opposite top*) AND 16 (*opposite bottom*). Early modern cartographers, from the sixteenth century through the eighteenth century, realized that their maps not only could convey knowledge about landforms but also could provide would-be explorers and traders with information about Natives and local resources. But as this example from the "Vallard" (Figure 15), which allegedly depicts the coast of Australia, and another from Herman Moll's early eighteenth-century map (Figure 16) reveal, the illustrations often represented idealized scenarios based on inexact evidence. San Marino, Huntington Library, HM 00029, http://www.digital-scriptorium.org. Library of Congress, Geography and Map Division.

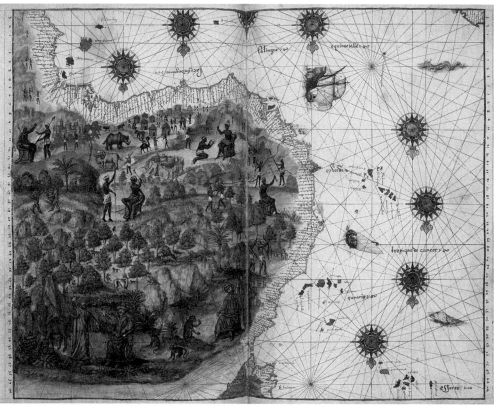

edges of the known world, including not only tales like Mandeville's but books such as the *Nuremberg Chronicle* of 1493, the last major reference work produced without any glimmer of knowledge about the Western Hemisphere.[29]

Maps, then, reflected their makers' understanding of what they knew and imaginary depictions of what they did not. They also revealed what was important to their patrons. The "Vallard Atlas" reflected the obsession of the cartographers of the Dieppe school with coastlines, evident throughout the work in the countless number of coastal toponyms. One coastline after the next is cluttered with place names, presumably drawn from Portuguese charts as they reflect Portuguese rendering of names.[30] Although one mapmaker included elaborate architecture in the interior of some of the European maps, he or she neglected to name places with any precision. London, for example, appears as an image of the Houses of Parliament. But the name of the city cannot be found on the map.[31] The mapmaker was instead concerned with depicting shoals and other maritime hazards far from Europe's western shores and occupying potential blank spaces with *mise en scènes* depicting human actions in exotic settings.

The "Vallard," like other sixteenth-century maps, provides a glimpse of a world in the process of change. Before 1492, the peoples of the Western Hemisphere, with the exception of Inuit, Beothuks, or

Mi'kmaqs, who met the small numbers of Norse sailors who had ventured across the North Atlantic, had no known contact with Europeans or Africans. Suddenly, in the century following Columbus's first voyage, Europeans bearing unknown fauna crossed the Atlantic. Most of them had two primary purposes: to pursue new economic or religious opportunities or to extract information about foreign places to support conquest. No one could have anticipated the ecological consequences that resulted from the voyages.

In 1972, the historian Alfred Crosby labeled the two-way movement of biota across the basin the "Columbian Exchange." The villains in his story, and in the similar histories that other scholars have written since, were infectious diseases. The scale of death, most of it likely caused by the spread of Old World illnesses, was never repeated in the Western Hemisphere after the seventeenth century. (Although epidemics of Eurasian diseases would continue to spread periodically until the nineteenth century, mortality rates never reached the levels of the first two hundred years of sustained contact.) The absence of easily quantifiable data makes it impossible to know exact mortality figures, but we can understand how the calamity occurred. Widespread death from smallpox, for example, followed enormous pressures put on Americans by European explorers and soldiers, whose collective actions fractured families, reduced available food supplies, and disrupted the workings of age-old economies. Under these circumstances, the pathogens brought by Europeans led to unprecedented mortality rates.[32]

Americans and Europeans recognized the link between the arrival of newcomers and the spread of death among Natives. To be sure, they did not have a modern concept of contagion and hence did not analyze epidemics as we do. But if sixteenth-century observers lacked a clinical vocabulary, Americans and Europeans alike witnessed the devastation caused by epidemics among Natives while the newcomers remained uninfected. Explanations for high death rates of indigenes differed from place to place. Sub-Arctic peoples saw the spread of infection as a repudiation of their sacred contract with the spirits of large game animals.[33] Carolina Algonquians believed that the English had brought invisible warriors with them who shot invisible bullets into native bodies—an apt visual metaphor for the irruption of smallpox pustules.[34] Europeans tended to have simpler explanations. Many believed that Natives died because God punished heathens, whereas Europeans survived because God favored them.[35] Only a few, such as the Spanish Franciscan chronicler Bernardino de Sahagún, recognized that death often resulted from the initial attack of a disease compounded by lack of sufficient palliative care. When writing about an epidemic of 1576, which raged while his team was constructing the last parts of the *Florentine Codex*, Sahagún noted "many died of hunger and from not having anyone to cure them nor provide what was necessary. It happened and happens in many homes, that all those of the house become sick without there being anyone who might offer a pitcher of water."[36] Modern observers have suggested that the devastating epidemic of 1576 was likely *cocoliztli*, a hemorrhagic fever that originated among rodents and spread more easily among the Mexica because of the Spanish conquest. Postcontact living conditions stressed Americans' bodies, making many more likely to perish from a disease that they might otherwise have survived. Indigenous therapies might have increased the lethal toll of an epidemic when swimming in a river was part of a traditional curing regimen, which could have led to drowning.[37]

The quick decline in indigenous populations acted as an accelerant for potential colonizers despite knowledge that the environment might be deadly and that cannibals and monsters might be lying in wait for unwary travelers. The earliest European stories about the bounties of American nature had come from Columbus himself. In his first report, published soon after his return, the explorer extolled the resources of the Caribbean islands he had visited. Hispaniola, he wrote in 1493, was "full of all kinds of trees, so tall they seem to touch the sky." The entire island was, he continued, "a marvel. Its sierras and mountains, it lowlands and meadows and its beautiful thick soil, are so apt for planting and sowing, for raising all kinds of cattle and for building towns." The local harbors were magnificent, and so were the "big rivers of good water, most of which carry gold." The islands boasted spices and cotton in unimaginable quantities. What is more, Columbus found people, thereby undermining the European belief that monsters roamed the margins of their world. To be sure, Columbus did mention rumors of an island populated by cannibals, but his readers would likely receive that news as the explorer himself did, convinced that such a custom was a cultural trait that could be eliminated and not a permanent characteristic of Americans.[38] Nonetheless, Europeans' belief in monsters crossed the Atlantic. Travelers' reports and maps supported the enduring belief by erasing the difference between monsters, on one hand, and the monstrous behavior of uncivilized people, on the other hand.

By the middle decades of the sixteenth century, European travel accounts routinely included details of regional resources and the potential profits to be extracted from American shores. The earliest accounts emanating from Brazil emphasized its natural bounty. Travelers used a strategy of analogous reading to describe what they saw, comparing American novelties with familiar scenes or objects from home. Europeans who read travel accounts or viewed the earliest paintings (such as those in the "Atlas Miller") and engravings would have found American nature simultaneously familiar and alluring. Dyers on the continent had long searched for sources of vibrant colors. That desire for profit fueled various reports, including the sections of the *Florentine Codex* that described the ways that certain American insects could be transformed into cochineal. (See Plate 3.) The desire for color also drove the passion for brazilwood, which appears across South America in the "Vallard Atlas." The atlas depicted

FIGURE 19. News about European explorers circulated rapidly on the continent, colliding with longstanding beliefs about what existed beyond Europe's borders. The Würzburg historian Lorenz Fries depicted dog-headed cynophali engaged in cannibalism. Fries also depicted a family of Javanese cannibals about to eat, various cannibals in the Americas, the "Terri canibalorū," and dog-headed creatures, dressed like humans, in Mongolia and Tartary. John Carter Brown Library.

naturalia of dazzling hues, including parrots and other Brazilian birds whose feathers already adorned Tupinambá headdresses. Europeans prized indigenous feather-work from both Brazil and Mexico even before the end of the century.[39] Nature could also dazzle in more mundane tones. As Léry wrote, sailors would not need to worry about lack of food during their journey to Brazil since flying fish leapt out of the water onto ships, a notion echoed in a 1592 edition of his book (see Figure 22).[40]

Stories about American abundance spread through Europe, crossing confessional lines. The possession of American nature came to be viewed as a reward in the ongoing religious contest between Protestants and Catholics, each of whom hoped to establish unassail-

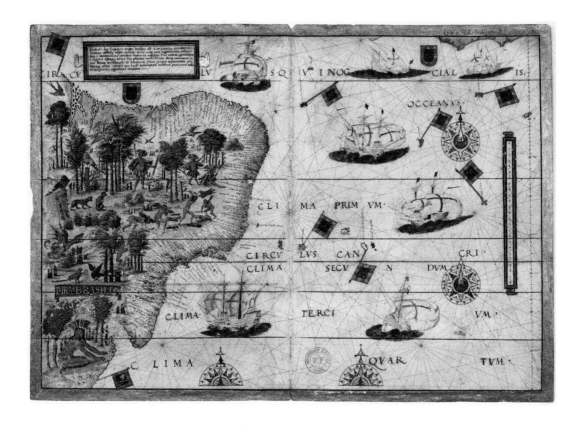

able claims to the Western Hemisphere. Propagandists on each side used the printing press to aid their efforts. Columbus's supporters struck first with the publication in 1493 of an account of his initial voyage, but other accounts soon followed, in ever-greater numbers.

After the Reformation, Protestants sought justification for their own American territory. The first English translation of Bartolomé de Las Casas's *Brief Account of the Destruction of the Indies*, first published in Seville in 1552, appeared in London in 1583 with the rather innocuous title *The Spanish Colonie*. Its contents provided English promoters of long-distance trade with ample evidence of Spanish perfidy—and added incentive to cross the Atlantic. In the hands of promoters like Hakluyt, establishing a major English presence in the Americas would simultaneously threaten the spread of Catholicism

FIGURES 20 (*opposite*) AND 21. European explorers in the sixteenth century always hunted for valuable commodities. This map, from the so-called "Atlas Miller" in Paris, suggests the commodities that Europeans could extract from the Western Hemisphere. Colonization would intensify the use of colors, evident here in the Tupinambás busily harvesting dyewood trees (characterized by the red bark) as well as the hue of birds hovering nearby, whose feathers resemble those on the headdresses worn by Tupinambás. Courtesy of the Bibliothèque Nationale and the National Museum of Copenhagen. (See Plates 4 and 5.)

and be a boon to the domestic economy. The year after the English translation of Las Casas's book appeared, Hakluyt sent a private document (known today as "The Discourse on Western Planting") to Queen Elizabeth I and her advisors. In the pages of that long manuscript, which he composed while a government spy in Paris, Hakluyt repeatedly chastised the Spanish and also enumerated the commodities to be extracted from the Western Hemisphere. Trying to convince the English to establish colonies across the Atlantic, he sang the praises of America's dense forests (so tempting to an island nation dependent on shipping), vast stocks of roaming animals, rivers choked with fish, and likely access via the as-yet undiscovered Northwest Passage to the South Sea and the riches of the Spice Islands. His argument had long-lasting consequences for the Americas.[41]

FIGURE 22. One European writer after another wrote about the Americas as containing a bounty that many could not have imagined existed. In addition to occasional comparisons to Eden, such texts also included particulars addressing anxieties felt by potential travelers. Jean de Léry, who did not shy from details about how foreign Americans could be, minimized lurking fears that the ride across the Atlantic would be difficult. He raved about the bounty to be found in the ocean. Of all aquatic resources, none was as incredible as the flying fish. When the workshop of Theodor de Bry produced an engraved edition of Léry's text fifteen years after it had initially been published, it included this remarkable image, which corresponded to Léry's claim that these creatures leapt onto the decks of passing ships, thereby providing an abundant source of food for travelers. Courtesy of the Huntington Library.

Over the course of the century, Spanish, Portuguese, French, and English ships sailed west seeking the resources of the Western Hemisphere and looking for new routes to the southwest Pacific and its magnificent bounty. Their quest for the South Sea was based on hard-won understanding of a geographic reality: cinnamon, cloves, nutmeg, mace, and peppers only came from distant locales with the proper climate. The desire to find a quick route to these tropical paradises intensified in the sixteenth century, which produced constant work for European cartographers trying to satisfy the demands of ship captains and explorers. In turn, returning sailors offered news about their experience to mapmakers and advocates of long-distance expeditions. They likely kept some things private, no doubt, but judging from the books emanating from print shops they had much to say about what they had observed.

The European encounter with the Western Hemisphere presented a series of challenges to mapmakers. In the sixteenth century, the most important information that a map gave explorers was how to find previously unknown lands. The shape of coastlines, the pattern of winds, the presence of dangerous shoals, the challenges of particular local climates, and the best possible places to anchor a ship were as important to arriving sailors as providing alluring details about the places they landed. But mapmakers, like everyone else in Europe, had relatively little information available about the Western Hemisphere. They had an especially difficult task reconciling popular ancient concepts, based on wisdom about the edges of the world, with news from recent journeys. They wanted to create a new map of the world—a map of a newly expanded nature—with limited knowledge and, despite the claims of promoters, enduring obstacles to overseas success.

Historians of cartography have emphasized that every map has a political purpose, whether we recognize it or not.[42] In the early mod-

ern Atlantic basin, European mapmakers often had very specific political goals—namely, identifying territory claimed by European explorers for their monarchs. These claims were often extravagant and
difficult to defend but useful for those who wanted to promote European conquest and colonization. For example, the map of the
Western Hemisphere in Sebastian Münster's mid-sixteenth-century
Cosmographia Universalis identified the range of Spanish and French
claims, which many French and Spanish had already asserted in other
documents. Since those places were already claimed by continental
Europeans, the English concentrated their energies on the mid-
Atlantic coast, from modern Maine to the northern boundary of La
Florida. While there were exceptions, such as Sir Francis Drake's
wanderings in the Orinoco in territory then claimed by Spain, Europeans typically put their efforts toward exploring, conquering, and
colonizing territory they believed they owned through an act of discovery. That notion ignored Native Americans' rights to their own
territory but did not dissuade cartographers eager to reveal the expanded territory controlled by their nation.

Following from such an idea, maps always constituted political
statements. The "Vallard" was no exception. Despite what might appear as its close attention to coastlines, its creators likely never intended it to be used at sea but instead, as two scholars have put it,
"to transmit an idea of the world" to Europeans at home.[43] As a result, these cartographers drew from contemporary efforts to understand nature on land and at sea. This is most evident in what may
seem at first the least remarkable map in the collection—a map of
the south Atlantic, with only bits of the Brazilian and African coasts
visible at its edges.[44] Although it is a depiction of a sea, it is far from
empty. The map has thirteen compass roses along its periphery and
another at the center. Each contains sixteen points, which allowed
for the calculation of thirty-two possible directions. Between north
and west, to take one example, one could calculate north by west,

north-northwest, northwest by north, northwest, west-northwest, west-northwest, and west by north. The idea was that navigators could use the tools they had on board—notably a compass (indicating north) and a measuring compass (to record distance), as well as navigational charts—to determine their location in open water. (Sailors could not measure longitude at sea until the development of an accurate clock known as a chronometer, which was invented in the eighteenth century.[45]) What is so special about this map? It is not a map of a place as much as a guide to figuring out wind patterns and currents, which were crucial for anyone who wanted to make a roundtrip journey that took them out of sight of land.[46] Its inclusion in the atlas testified to a quest for knowledge that went well beyond depicting continental interiors.

Obsession with wind patterns was not limited to Europeans. Inuit, to take one American example, paid close attention to wind patterns because the direction of the winds influenced local weather conditions. There were words that signified the direction of the wind (*kannernark* indicated a northwest wind while *niggierk* referred to one from the southeast) and its power.[47] Inuit of Nunavut sang to the spirits who controlled the seas, including winds that could propel or imperil a voyager. Long exposure to the fierce hurricanes of the Caribbean had led Mesoamericans to integrate gods of wind into their belief systems. Taíno cosmology includes tales of ancient winds so powerful that, as the historian Stuart Schwartz has written, they had "separated the Virgin Islands and the Bahamas from Cuba, and their force continued to shape the contours of the island world."[48]

Everyone who sailed the ocean needed to learn about prevailing wind patterns in order to improve their chances for survival. Christians across Europe had for centuries pleaded with saints to bring them favorable weather, including winds to propel them to their destination (or to keep their enemies away). The Swedish cleric

Olaus Magnus, who in 1555 composed a lengthy and influential treatise on the peoples of the north, was convinced that the Finns had
magical powers to summon the winds. As he wrote, "There was a
time when the Finns, among other pagan delusions, would offer
wind for sale to traders who were detained on their coasts by off-
shore gales, and when payment had been brought would give them
in return three magic knots tied in a strap not likely to break." Each
knot had a particular power. When the merchants "undid the first
they would have gentle breezes; when they unloosed the second the
winds would be stiffer; but when they untied the third they must
endure such raging gales that, their strength exhausted, they would
have no eye to look out for rocks from the bow, nor a footing either
in the body of the ship to strike the sails or at the stern to guide the
helm." In other words, they would succumb to the power of the
wind and their ships would be destroyed.[49]

The "Vallard" creators might have cared about where winds came
from, but their dominant concern was where they would take someone. The places that the mapmakers presumably knew best—the
southern coasts of Europe, the northern coast of Africa, and the
shores of the Adriatic and the Aegean—are filled with toponyms
derived from Portuguese and Venetian maps. Shorn of the need to
provide the number of places identified in the larger map of Europe,
these maps, particularly of the two seas, dwell on local communities.
The artist also drew on knowledge of contemporary politics to create images. The Grand Turk—Suleiman the Magnificent during the
time of the creation of the atlas—is the largest figure on any of the
maps, a sign of his power.[50]

By contrast, maps for Africa and especially the Americas displayed more illustrations other than interior toponyms. The Aztec
capital of Tenochtitlan (on folio 10) could be identified easily because the "Vallard Atlas" depicts it in the middle of a great lake with
causeways connecting to large buildings on its periphery, a visual

Dye figur anzaigt vns das volck vnd infel die gefunden ist durch den christenlichen künig zu Portigal oder von seinen vnterthonen. Die leüt sind also nacket hübsch, braun wolgestalt von leib, ir heübt hals, arm, scham, füß, frawen vnd mann ain wenig mit federn bedeckt. Auch haben die mann in iren angesichten vnd brust vil edel gestain. Es hat auch nyemann nichts sunder sind alle ding gmain vnd die mann habendt weyber welche in gefallen, es sey müter, schwester oder freündt, darinn haben sy kain vnderscheyd. Sy streyten auch mit einander. Sy essen auch ainander selbs die erschlagen werden, vnd hencken das selbig flaisch in den rauch. Sy werden alt hundert vnd fünftzig iar. Vnd haben kain regiment.

FIGURE 23. By the time the illustrators of the "Vallard" came to decorate their maps of Brazil, images of the region's Natives had already circulated for at least a generation. This 1505 broadside, one of the rarest surviving early images of Brazil, provided the earliest visual representation of the Tupinambás for European viewers. The picture established many of the visual and literary tropes that would dominate European views of Tupinambás throughout the sixteenth century, including graphic evidence of the alleged practice of cannibalism. Courtesy of The New York Public Library. Spencer Collection, The New York Public Library, Astor, Lenox, and Tilden Foundations.

description derived from contemporary European writing about Moctezuma's famed city. The picture of Brazil (on folio 12) reveals Europeans engaged in both trade and hostilities with locals, presumably Tupinambás. One visitor offers a mirror to an indigenous leader (distinguished by his feather headdress, similar to a 1505 print of Tupinambás that had been published in Augsburg) while another wields a sword nearby. The encounter is worth a close look not only because it suggests the importance of commerce but because the Tupinambás offer captive monkeys bound by red leashes and green parrots perched on their arms. The European had come with the tools of his civilization, including a basket of weapons and a mirror, eager to take American fauna in exchange.

The maps in the "Vallard" did not depict the Western Hemisphere as a newfound Eden, although of course some Europeans did evoke that idea in written works of the sixteenth century. In addition to Columbus believing that he might have located the entrance to the terrestrial paradise, Theodor de Bry inserted an illustration of Adam and Eve into his 1590 edition of Thomas Harriot's *Briefe and True Report of the Newfound Land of Virginia*.[51] But the cartographers in Dieppe had another idea in mind. The same map that depicted peaceful trade between Europeans and Tupinambás in Brazil also revealed a battle being fought, rather improbably, between naked foes somewhere on the south side of the Straights of Magellan, likely the mythic Patagonian giants described by Antonio Pigafetta, the chronicler of Magellan's circumnavigation a generation earlier.[52] A second image (on folio 11) reveals a priest bleeding from the head as Natives nearby set up a fire—quite likely to roast him for dinner, a reference to American cannibalism that appeared on other maps from the Dieppe school, including Rotz's. Indigenous people on the map also kill other Natives, including a group of archers, their quivers filled with arrows, who have brought down a man bleeding profusely from his wounds (also on folio 11).

A viewer of the "Vallard" might have noticed, too, that the Americans on these maps were more intimate with nature than Europeans. With the exception of the depiction of Tenochtitlan, which looks as glorious as most cities of the Old World in this atlas,[53] Americans primarily seem to live without many permanent abodes. They stroll, mostly naked, through a wondrous landscape. The European man who offers a mirror to a group of Tupinambás is one of only two individuals—the other is also European—wearing clothing in that scene. The headman with whom he is negotiating has turned his head away from the European and is gesturing to his companions, with a finger pointing toward the newcomer as if to suggest it is time to trade American goods for the visitor's tools but not his garments.

Scenes across this map show human activity. The Americans never just lounge lazily. They use bows and arrows to hunt, carry chopped lumber, and sow crops, likely cotton—although it is possible that they are tending rice transported from West Africa on Portuguese ships, which quickly became a staple crop in the region.[54] The only notable exception is a man sitting down, with one hand covering his face. That pose was not coincidental: Europeans typically depicted Tupinambás striking such a pose, which indicated either mourning or, more likely in this instance, welcome. According to modern anthropologists, the Tupinambá welcoming gesture looked like mourning because the Americans were anticipating the eventual departure of their visitors and hence wanted to express their impending sadness.[55] Nature is wilder in these scenes than in the Old World, but Americans showed Europeans how to extract what they wanted from it.

The display of nature in the "Vallard" was erratic. As in other atlases and charts produced in mid-century Dieppe, the mapmaker paid no attention to the Arctic or made any effort to depict possible northern passages. The "Vallard" does not include Greenland, well known to Europeans by then, and has only a cursory image of Iceland, although the cartographer did present a detailed view of the coastlines of Labrador and Newfoundland, as well as many place names along the St. Lawrence River. The mapmaker was careful to demarcate shoals in these northern waters, too, once again conveying information that would be of most use to European sailors.[56]

Curiously, of the five images that depict the Western Hemisphere, none shows Americans taking advantage of marine resources. The only vessels at sea are those built by Europeans. It would be too much to expect that the Dieppe cartographers would understand the ecological rhythms of all Americans, who in some places moved to river valleys and coastlines during parts of the year to harvest fish and shellfish.[57] Still, to suggest that Americans depended on land-based flora and fauna reveals a decided lack of interest in certain details available in travel narratives that the mapmakers used to render their two-dimensional depictions of the world. To these mapmakers, the sea was a place to be crossed, not a resource to be harvested, even though Europeans had for generations been extracting aquatic riches from the North American continental shelf and other Atlantic ecosystems.[58]

Mapmakers chose to show that only Europeans could command the seas for both political and ideological ends. By revealing European prowess, the Dieppe cartographers reinforced the idea already circulating by the middle of the sixteenth century that Europeans came from more advanced civilizations than Americans. As they conceived the situation, their science and technology enabled them to visit and exploit every region of the globe while most Americans, with the notable exception of the residents of Tenochtitlan, lived in rude dwellings and harnessed nothing more than monkeys. The fantasy of Pope Alexander VI's 1493 papal bull "Inter Caetera" and the 1494 Treaty of Tordesillas, which divided the Western Hemisphere between Spain and Portugal, rested on the presumption of European Christian superiority over indigenous claims to territory, an act as political as it was religious.[59] The decision to leave Americans out of the sea had a similar ideological component. From the start, artists had used imagery to establish technological superiority. The anonymous depiction of Columbus confronting Tainos in a 1493 woodcut reveals the Spanish as the owners of a complicated sailing vessel meeting an indigenous population apparently incapable of building such a ship or even of clothing themselves. The Dieppe school pushed that idea farther. Europeans, the creator of the "Vallard" and other mapmakers demonstrated, were the only ones both able and interested in extracting the resources that lay beneath the waves.

But what did the sea mean to the maker of the "Vallard"? Unlike other sixteenth-century European maps, such as those produced soon after by the northern cartographers Abraham Ortelius and Gerardus Mercator, the seas in the "Vallard" are calm. The mapmaker depicted a grand total of three aquatic creatures on the map of the south Atlantic: two fish with teeth and what appears to be a large sea serpent trolling the waters off the west coast of Africa. Curiously, the artist painted six Tupinambás at the water's edge, one of them improbably drawing back his bow to launch an arrow into the ocean toward an unseen target.[60] The creator of the "Vallard" did not care about the water but its edges. This was, after all, an atlas of coastlines, not an effort to re-create nature. A mariner would learn more about shoals than shellfish here.

The "Vallard" provided viewers with a large-scale, selective, and impressionistic view of nature in the Americas and elsewhere. In this sense, it differs from the "Histoire Naturelle des Indes," also known as the "Drake Manuscript," which is in the possession of the Morgan Library. The work, like the "Vallard," is by one or two unknown hands and dates from the late sixteenth century, likely the 1590s.[61]

The creators of the "Histoire Naturelle" concentrated on illustrating unique flora, a wise choice since sixteenth-century Europeans were always eager to find new plants to satisfy their medicinal and gastric demands.[62] The manuscript contains pictures of one plant after another—West Indian garlic, icaco (coco plum), avocado, berries, pineapples, gourds, tomatoes, sweet potatoes, coconuts, plantains, watermelon, cactus, and figs. Unlike later scientific observers, who were eager to classify plants in relation to others based on their morphological structure, these sixteenth-century observers were more concerned with the uses of plants.[63] They pro-

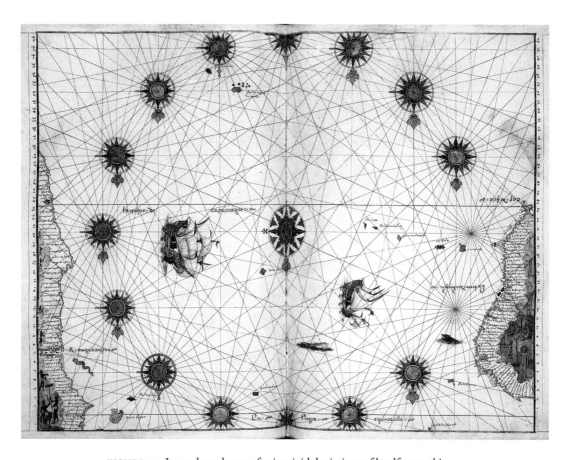

FIGURE 24. In a volume known for its vivid depictions of landforms, this map of the South Atlantic Ocean seems an oddity. The artist depicted only small slices of West Africa (on the left in this southward-oriented map) and Brazil (on the right) but, more surprisingly, opted not to fill the seas with creatures of one shape or another, which had already become a common tradition of European mapmakers. Instead, the artist filled the page with compass roses and rhomb lines, devices that were of use to people at sea or, in this instance, perhaps designed to suggest sufficient understanding of wind patterns to justify the expense of long-distance explorations. San Marino, Huntington Library, HM 00029. http://www.digital-scriptorium.org.

vided brief descriptions for each specimen, often comparing them to plants known in Europe. Readers learned that "*ache des yndes*" or "garlic of the Indies" was "sweeter than the garlic to be found in France. It stays together and does not separate at all on touch like that of France. The Indians are very fond of it; they roast it on the fire like a pear and eat it." Pineapples, the manuscript noted, were "eaten raw with salt only to relive the Indians of stomach pains." Squash grew from seeds that the locals planted. "They live on this fruit," the author added, "letting it roast on their wood fires; it is excellent food for the Indians and there is plenty of it." Sweet potatoes were especially intriguing. "The Indians use this fruit as excellent nourishment and cook it with meat in a pot or braise it," the observer noted; "it originates in the earth; is shaped like a root, and one can multiply it by cutting small pieces which one plants like a seed which grows."[64]

Tobacco, which had already captured the attention of Europeans who believed that it could cure virtually every human ailment, got extensive treatment. News about the plant's medicinal powers had by then spread across the continent, most notably in a treatise from a Seville-based physician named Nicolás Monardes, who described many of the health-giving wonders to be found in the Western Hemisphere. The book appeared first in two volumes in Seville, published in 1569 and 1571, then emerged across the continent: two Italian editions came from Venetian presses, one in 1582 and the next in 1597, and the English version, published in London in 1577, appeared again in 1580 and in 1596 with the optimistic title *Joyfull Newes out of the Newfound World*. While Europeans had an interest in plants in general, which printers tried to meet with the publication of vast herbals containing centuries of botanical information supplemented by new illustrations, tobacco became the rage, in part because it attracted both advocates and opponents. Books and pamphlets advanced arguments for and against its use.[65]

The "Histoire Naturelle" constituted a new report from the American field. The manuscript noted that indigenous peoples of the Caribbean used tobacco "for food as well as an extremely beneficial medicine." "When they are sick," the text continued, "they breathe in the smoke by mouth with a straw; soon the ill humour escapes by vomiting." For tobacco to be effective, it needed to be crushed. "They often pulverize it and, putting it in their noses, it distills several drops of water from the brain to discharge it." Suffering from a toothache? Lay the leaves of tobacco on the tooth and "the pain disappears." Eye problems? Soak the leaves in water and then use them to bathe one's eyes.[66]

Such details had become commonplace in Europe by then. But the creators of the "Histoire Naturelle" added a fresh image of healers wielding tobacco to mend a grievous injury. As the manuscript noted, "When the Indians are mortally wounded by arrows, one lays them on a rack and makes an oven with a tube leading to the wound of the sick man. When the fire is lighted, they put in it a leaf of tobacco together with a resin called balsam and as soon as the smoke enters the wound of the patient, they take a leaf of tobacco with some of the balsam and make a plaster which they apply to the wound of the patient, and he is cured."[67]

The description and the image conveyed a specific message: the West Indies was the home to a marvelous and valuable plant with countless uses. Those who cultivated it could share secrets about how best to extract its medicinal properties. This seems obvious enough from the picture and an elaboration of ways Europeans could use the plant. But not all images were so positive. De Bry's workshop engraved a memorable image of tobacco use among the Tupinambás in Brazil. They dance in a circle, half-clad, heavily tattooed with the points of feathers embedded in their skin, around three men who are blowing tobacco smoke. This picture, along with the accounts of travelers, pointed to a practical problem: if Americans employed tobacco in pagan rituals, how could Europeans know it was safe for Christians? Could it, as some prominent Europeans—including, in the early seventeenth century, the future king of England[68]—thought, undermine Europeans by corrupting those who consumed it? Those who promoted the sale of the sot weed relied on information like that in the "Histoire Naturelle" and other practical accounts of tobacco that depicted the medical benefits of the plant without making suggestive links to heathen rites.

Page after page, the "Histoire Naturelle" revealed how Americans profited from their lush surroundings. The manuscript explained how strong storms deluged the mountains, creating streams that brought gold and fresh water to those below. One leaf of the manuscript revealed how the locals caught fish using spears, nets, and lines they dragged from their canoes, looping these cords over their ears and in their mouths so that they could immediately feel the pull of the fish. Americans, the text revealed, had mastered this environment, on land as well as sea. They figured out how to spin cotton to make fine cloth, and they set elaborate traps in trees to catch parrots. Some became so adept at holding their breath that they could spend—so the authors claimed—up to fifteen minutes under water harvesting pearls. The deeper they went, so the manuscript noted, the larger the pearls, thereby providing new raw materials for a global market.[69]

Such details reflected an awareness of nature that fascinated Europeans. Since the early decades of the century, they had heard stories about Americans using fireflies to guide their way through forests at night and a Mexican ruler who could summon a manatee to carry him or his friends across open water—but refused to haul any Europeans after being wounded by one of them.[70] Many Europeans became fascinated with the variegated colors of birds and the feather-work produced by locals. Mexica feather-work fascinated Sahagún as well. One sixteenth-century codex contains a series of images detailing the ways that Americans worked with feathers to produce works of art that might be displayed on a tapestry. Vividly colored Tupinambá feather headdresses inspired European artists, who repeatedly depicted them on maps.[71]

HINDE · FLECHER ·

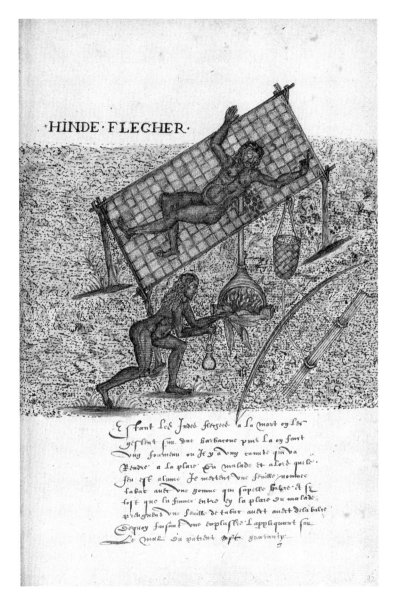

Estant Les Jndes flecces a La mort oy Lee
gesslent sur Dne barbarone pme La oy font
Dny fourneau ou Je y a Dny camité qui Da
Vendre a La plare ou malade et alors quele
feu est alume Je mettent Dne feuille nommee
tabat auec Dne gomme qui sapelle faltre et se
soit que lu fumee entre Ley la plare ou malade
prennent Dne feuille de tabat auec auct dela bulte
Dequoy fasant Dne emplastre L appliquant sur
Le mal du patient est guerenuy.

FIGURES 25 (*opposite*) AND 26 (*above*). Europeans fell in love with tobacco, a plant indigenous across the Western Hemisphere but in no other part of the world, for both the pleasure of its consumption and its alleged health bene-fits. Yet while European physicians could tell readers how to apply tobacco in various instances, few pictures showed how it worked. The image in Figure 25, which was perhaps never reprinted until the late twentieth century, would have likely caught the attention of readers had it been circulated. Here was proof, in a seemingly reliable report from the field, of the miraculous powers of a plant that would eventually play a major role in global commerce. Of course, other visual information circulated as well, including the de Bry work-shop's rendering of a Tupinambá ritual (above) witnessed (in the top right corner) by three visiting Europeans. Courtesy of the Morgan Library and the Huntington Library.

· CANA·DECOÍ LES HINDES·
· VONT·ALA·PAÍCHERÍE·
Et Comme Ilz pesschent le poisson

Vont A la mie auec leur canau et signé amaran
Leur ligne a eng dru cosfig du Canau Cela eslam fait
prennent leurs lignes et les mettent sur leurs auteilles
et lautre a leur bouche puis sentam que le poisson est
pris promptinem aus leurs mains tirem leur ligne
et le poisson

FIGURE 27. Americans inhabiting the Caribbean had always relied on the sea
for nutrition. Over time, some of these peoples, including the unidentified
islanders depicted here, developed sophisticated strategies for catching fish.
In this scene, one of the locals shows how one could use a fine thread to signal
that a fish had tugged on a line. Courtesy of the Morgan Library.

FIGURE 28. Brazilwood trees with their bright red cores and Tupinambá feather headdresses each testified to the vibrant colors to be found in Brazil in the sixteenth century. This image from the "Atlas Miller" of 1519 evokes an indigenous lumber business as well as showing the abundant colorful avian species whose plumage provided the material basis for Tupinambá head-dresses, shields, and garments. Courtesy of the Bibliothèque Nationale.

VACHE·BRAVE·

FIGURES 29 (*above*) AND 30 (*opposite*). Europeans believed that American
nature contained unlimited bounty. But just as tobacco could be dangerous
with uncontrolled use, so American fauna could punish the unwary. The cai-
man could kill quickly and, if the creator of the manuscript is to be believed,
American deer could tempt European bulls to mate and produce wild
unmanageable cattle. Courtesy of the Morgan Library.

To triumph in America, the newcomers recognized, they would need to acquire the knowledge of the Natives. Such information was crucial for any initial success the newcomers sought. But the "Histoire Naturelle" also depicted a place already changing as a result of the arrival of Europeans. The book contained information about wheat grown on the mainland and described a deep-water port found by Spanish visitors. It portrayed transported Africans working in mines in Peru and described trade that sent American wheat from new colonies to the Canary Islands in exchange for wine and metal fishhooks.[72] Taken together, the images and text reveal how new economic regimes, dictated by Europeans, were altering the landscape of the islands and nearby territory on the mainland. Among the novelties was a feral cow, purportedly produced from a bull and a deer—a new species for an emerging world.

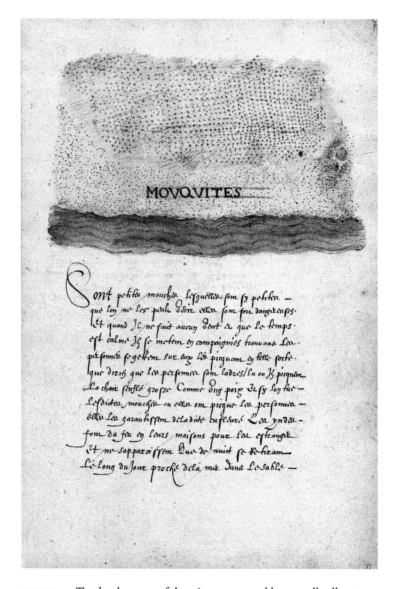

FIGURE 31. The development of the microscope would eventually allow Europeans to provide detailed views of very small things, but in the sixteenth-century Caribbean, there was no way to get a clear image of a mosquito, at least not for a visiting artist who had never experienced the pests before. The image here conveys the uniqueness of American mosquitoes, which seemed to come in invisible hordes, to torture their human prey. Courtesy of the Morgan Library. (See Plate 9.)

Eventually, Europeans would gain control of the Caribbean basin and much of the American mainland, but they had not yet done so by the end of the sixteenth century. The "Histoire Naturelle" contains an illustration of one island populated entirely by caimans and turtles; its lack of fresh water made it uninhabitable for humans but an ideal hunting ground for those seeking fresh meat. More revealing still was an image that might seem the least useful of all in the "Histoire Naturelle": a picture, consisting of nothing more than small, undefined insects swarming over a body of water, labeled "Mouquites"—mosquitoes. "They are small flies which are so small that one cannot see them, they are very dangerous," the unknown author wrote. "When there is no wind and the weather is calm, they come in droves attacking people, stinging them in such a manner that one would take them for lepers. Where they bite, the flesh swells up like a pea and if one kills said flies where they have stung, this protects them from the swelling." The tormenters attacked only at night. The locals knew what to do: build a fire in a house and the smoke would keep them away.[73] Such a trick would have appealed to European explorers, who were tortured by biting insects as far north as the Arctic.[74]

Maps and drawings served notice that a new environment was taking shape in the Atlantic basin. Old World commodities, like fishhooks and mirrors, could be found in increasing number in American communities. European captains made sure to pack the holds of their returning eastward-bound ships with American flora and fauna, along with as many pearls or emeralds or as much gold as possible. Some transported brazilwood so that it could be replanted, as occurred in Rouen in the 1550s, where local enthusiasts created a faux Brazilian panorama for King Henri II. Recognizing the lure of

FIGURE 32. A brazilwood sign that hung over the portal of a merchant's establishment in Rouen in the mid-sixteenth century. European dye makers understood the singular properties of brazilwood for its use in their trade. But as this sign reveals, they also wanted to display their mastery of a new product that, many hoped, they would eventually grow domestically. Musée départemental des Antiquités de la Seine-Maritime Rouen.

this tree, one local merchant had a sign carved depicting the stages of harvesting brazilwood.[75]

During the sixteenth century, Europeans understood that success depended on understanding nature. Before the Old and New Worlds met, that had meant trying to harness the powers of the divine. In an age of rapidly changing ecosystems, Americans and Europeans alike needed to adapt in ways that neither had anticipated before 1492.

CHAPTER THREE

The Landscape of History

Between 1492 and 1600, thousands of Europeans crossed the Atlantic Ocean. They came from different political regimes and confessional traditions. They traveled to the frigid Arctic and to stifling tropics. They encountered indigenous Americans who relied on the sea for sustenance and others who had mastered maize agriculture and hence could store enough food to sustain large cities. Some native peoples knew every creature that roamed local woods or high grasses on the edge of their settlements—and knew how to find the beasts by following tracks in the snow, setting fires to herd them into killing fields or off cliffs, or attending to the deities who controlled the animals' movements. Americans knew the seasons and how and where to find what they needed to survive and flourish, drawing on detailed collective memories to generate mental maps that were never sketched or written.[1]

Yet despite the obvious presence of complex cultures in the Western Hemisphere, Europeans remained convinced that they had a legitimate claim to Americans' land, which they intended to appropriate so that they could put it to the uses dictated by the Christian God. The notion developed immediately in 1492. Columbus told Ferdinand and Isabella that he had "discovered a great many islands inhabited by people without number: and of them all I have taken possession on behalf of Their Highnesses by proclamation and with the royal flag extended, and I was not opposed." He proceeded to rename every place he visited.[2] Soon after, Pope Alexander VI, who was born near Valencia, mandated the division of the Western Hemisphere between Spain and Portugal.

Eventually, other Europeans embraced the notion that they could lay claim to already settled lands. In 1629, 137 years after Columbus had first landed, the English Puritan John Winthrop, shortly before sailing across the ocean where he would become the governor of Massachusetts, argued that the English had a legitimate right to settle where Natives lived because the Americans did not possess what he considered to be a perfect title to the land. They had a right of occupation, to be sure, which Winthrop called a "natural right" to the places where they dwelled. But since Americans moved seasonally across large territories and, more crucially, kept no domesticated livestock and did not fence their lands, they had not earned what he labeled a "civil right" to their own homeland. That notion of property ownership was embedded, Winthrop argued, in scripture, which endowed the English claims with historical, legal, and religious legitimacy.[3]

Winthrop's testimony revealed the underlying motivation in most of the early European observers' accounts. He was not concerned with explicating Americans' understanding of the environment they had shaped over many generations. Instead, he believed the time had come to clarify these English migrants' claims to already peopled territory. Like other European writers, he saw the Natives' lands as untouched by human settlements and thus were empty—*vacuum domicilium*, without the marks of humans—and hence available for newcomers who would use land as their sacred texts proscribed.[4]

Wherever they arrived, Europeans mapped and marked Americans' lands. They enacted different rituals for claiming their territory, yet they all sought to justify colonization and mark their territory as unavailable to other potential claimants.[5] Visual evidence often furthered this agenda. Of the four major maps of the Western Hemisphere in the "Vallard Atlas," only one marks an American city—Tenochtitlan, which by then had already figured prominently in Spanish writings.[6] By the early seventeenth century, Europeans did not question their right to claim American lands; instead, they argued with each other over which European polity could assert ownership of specific territories in the Western Hemisphere and elsewhere beyond Europe. That dispute lay behind the efforts of the Dutch legal theorist Hugo Grotius, whose *Mare Liberum* of 1609 laid out an intellectual justification for northern European Protestants gaining entry to the Spice Islands, as well as the polymath John Dee's ambitious design for English expansion into North America.[7]

Europeans marked land on their maps as their possession through the rights conferred by discovery. They planted their flags, cleared fields, and erected fences. In 1614, men accompanying the English explorer William Baffin raised the standard of King James and erected a cross in Spitsbergen and also, as one chronicler wrote, took "a piece of Earth, as a sign of lawful possession." In 1621 the English captain Thomas James, having explored the body of water where Henry Hudson had spent the winter of 1610–1611, erected a cross with a note attached claiming that region for King James and Queen Henrietta Maria, and he also added English place names to their maps even though these locales had earlier been named by local Crees.[8]

Europeans also kidnapped Natives and sailed home to display them, transporting American bodies in a kind of synecdoche for acquiring American land.[9] As early as the 1490s, the Venetian explorers John and Sebastian Cabot, sailing with the support of the English monarch, took Inuit captives who later could be seen walking through Westminster dressed like Englishmen.[10] One hundred years later, a chronicler of the Arctic explorer Martin Frobisher, who also captured and displayed Inuit captives, believed that the kidnapping of Natives by the Cabots enabled the English to establish a right to much of the North Atlantic.[11]

Advocates of overseas expansion also circulated images among European audiences advertising their claims to American soil. This strategy was particularly successful for the English who claimed the outer banks of modern North Carolina. Images generated by the English painter John White in 1585, which were subsequently reinterpreted and engraved in the Frankfurt workshop of the Flemish engraver Theodor de Bry and published in 1590 in the four-language edition of Thomas Harriot's *Briefe and True Report of the New Found Land of Virginia*, played a decisive role in promoting English plans for colonizing eastern North America.

There has been no shortage of scholarly commentary on White's images and de Bry's engravings of them. Art historians have analyzed the style of these images, noting that the engraving techniques employed in the de Bry workshop established the savagery of the Americas and also located Americans in a recognizable visual tradition based on Renaissance portraiture techniques (although White's pictures at times seem less formal than de Bry's).[12] Literary critics have scrutinized the book to explain its place among early modern English travel accounts.[13] One botanist used the de Bry engraving of Secota to prove that the Algonquians cultivated sunflowers, while an ornithologist employed White's drawing of the town to explain indigenous efforts to prevent crows from raiding cornfields.[14] Other scholars have written about the paintings as objects, recounting their history—including the sorry saga of the Earl of Charlemont, who had sent them to Sotheby's for sale in the late eighteenth century but where water from a fire brigade soaked them during a warehouse fire in the mid-nineteenth century.[15] Historians have focused on the story of the engravings and the role that these images played in the development of the de Bry workshop, as well as the utility of these images as propaganda for English colonizing ventures.[16] Others have used the images to summarize the European arrival in North America, ignoring the potential of these images to mark a singular historical moment for the Carolina Algonquians.[17]

While it is true that the early images of these Algonquian communities should not necessarily be seen as accurate representations of indigenous Carolina society, the pictures do depict a transitional moment for this group of Americans. In some sense, the history of the images themselves parallels that very transition, particularly the changes that de Bry made in his engravings of White's watercolors of the town of Secota. The paintings reveal a European artist's view of an American people's manipulation of its environment to create a successful society and economy integrated into the world of the spirits. The engravings shaped the English idea of the region as a place where colonizers could find economic profit and bring Natives to civilization via conversion to English-style religion and social practices.

The first English to arrive on the North American mainland with plans to stay for a while—unlike, for example, the exploratory groups that made it to Nunavut in 1576 and Newfoundland in 1583[18]—extolled the virtues of the Carolina environment in language that evoked the biblical paradise. The younger Hakluyt published the accounts of travelers to Carolina among other expedition narratives in part to convince his countrymen to establish colonies in eastern North America.[19]

Most of the explorers' writings in Hakluyt's books could be read, as he intended them to be, as promotional. The North America described in his pages was indeed inviting. "The soil is the most plentifull, sweete, fruitfull, and wholsome of all the world," the English captains Philip Amadas and Arthur Barlowe wrote about coastal Carolina in 1584. The people were just as welcoming. Amadas and Barlowe wrote that the Algonquians tended to all their needs—feeding the newcomers and even washing their clothes and their feet "in warme water," the kind of small detail sure to lodge in the memory of a potential migrant. "We were entertained with all love, and kindness, and with as much bountie, after their manner, as they could possibly devise," they continued. "Wee found the people most gentle, loving, and faithfull, void of all guile and treason, and such as lived after the manner of the golden age. The earth bringeth foorth all things in aboundance, as in the first creation, without toile or labour."[20]

Although Amadas and Barlowe explained what they saw in scriptural terms, using a rhetorical device that later English migrants would employ consistently, their intent was to offer an accurate portrait of an inviting place. This was a new Eden, or could be. The English knew there were dangers in the Americas, of course, from reading travel accounts that warned about cannibals and monsters.[21] By the 1580s, there was also abundant information circulating in Europe about the bounty to be extracted in the Western Hemisphere, often framed in comparison to European commodities to render American nature more recognizable. Images of American settlements in Europeans' books or on their maps rendered parts of the indigenous landscape more intelligible to those who had spent their lives in or near cities.[22]

FIGURES 33 (*opposite top*) AND 34 (*opposite bottom*). Europeans often wrote as if they were descending into a lightly settled wilderness, but mapmakers often knew better. Americans might not have had many cities, but some at least lived in settlements recognizable to Europeans. Hochelaga (Figure 33, present-day Montreal) and Tenochtitlan (Figure 34, modern Mexico City) were the most prominent and so merited attention in works intended to provide information about the Western Hemisphere, including the "Vallard Atlas" as well as the better-known *Navigationi et Viaggi* by the Venetian civil servant Giovanni Battista Ramusio. Courtesy of the Huntington Library.

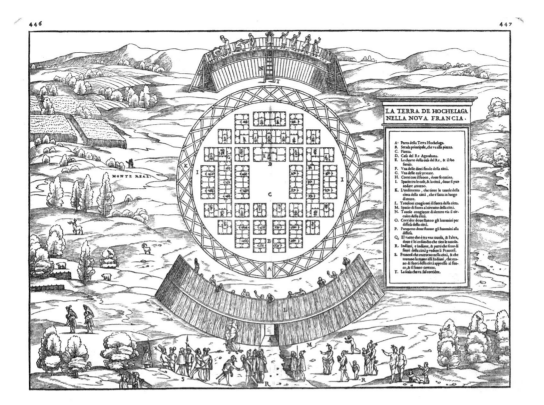

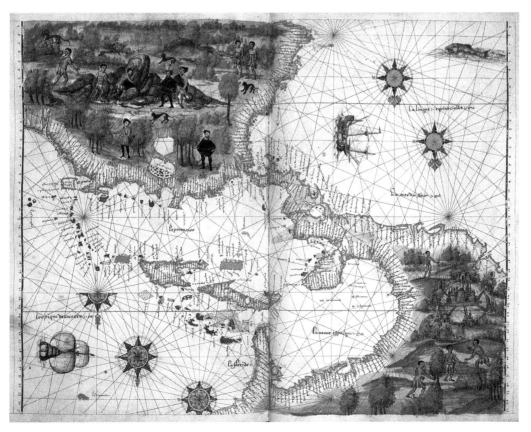

Yet how were European audiences to reconcile an American history evident in planned cities with the notion that Americans inhabited an ageless Eden? Hakluyt and others realized that they had to square claims about an American Paradise with a concept of cultural evolution that situated the peoples and settlements along the Carolina coast at a particular moment in the progress of humanity. This required a biblical framework, a deep understanding of the Algonquians and their culture, and a systematic effort to spread news about this place and its peoples to potential supporters of colonization. These demands motivated Hakluyt and his partners to create the 1590 edition of Harriot's account, which remained in circulation long after the so-called lost colonists had disappeared into the mists of time.

To understand how to read the pictures from the outer banks, we need to understand the context of their creation. In 1585, a skilled artist named John White and the young mathematician Thomas Harriot arrived in North America as part of an English expedition to territory claimed by Queen Elizabeth I. White painted a series of watercolors of local peoples and resources. In all likelihood, White traveled west with the idea that he would, as an artist on a journey to Newfoundland in 1582 had been instructed, "drawe to liefe all strange birdes beastes fishes plantes hearbes Trees and fruictes and bring home of each sorte as nere as you may. Also drawe the figures & shapes of men and woemen in their apparel as also of their manner of wepons in every place as you shall finde them differing."[23] The absence of any directions for White as well as the loss of the original drawings makes it impossible to know with certainty his precise goals when he was in Carolina.[24]

White and Harriot soon returned to England. In 1588, Harriot published his *Briefe and True Report* in 1588. In 1589, Hakluyt included Harriot's text in his own extensive collection of travel narratives, published as *Principall Navigations, Voiages, and Discoveries of the English Nation*. In 1590, the de Bry workshop in Frankfurt-am-Main produced four versions of Harriot's book—in Latin, English, French, and German—with engravings based on White's paintings. De Bry had by then spent time in London, where it is likely that he either acquired the watercolors or made arrangements to have some selection of them sent to his atelier.[25]

Nine of the workshop's twenty-three engravings depicted individuals while the rest illustrated either the Algonquians' daily activities or their buildings and communities. Yet the engravings do not mimic the paintings. White set his figures into stark white backgrounds as if they were studies for portraits that would be fully imagined in an artist's London studio. The engravers, for their part, took the figures and set them into fictional landscapes, thereby offering a non-eyewitness version of the environment and the locals' use of it. For example, the picture of a "weroan or great Lorde of Virginia" also depicted a hunting scene, while the printed book's facing image of a "chief lady" included a view of fishing and, deeper in the background, a man shooting an arrow into a deer. As it turns out, scenes of the coastline or rivers appeared time and again in these portraits, reinforcing Harriot's statement that the Algonquians developed an economy that relied on aquatic resources. Even the engraving of a local medicine man, labeled "the flyer" by White and "the Conjurer" by de Bry, shows flocks of birds being hunted with canoes and a deer fleeing as two hunters pursue it.[26]

The remaining images in de Bry's publication show, in one way or another, Algonquian uses of diverse local resources. In one engraving, two men burn out the inside of a tree to make a canoe; that same shallow craft appears in the following image, which illustrates the bounty of the coastal region and the Natives' multiple fishing techniques. The Algonquians were skilled fishermen, as the image of them "broiling of their fishe over the flame" reveals. They were farmers as well; the book contains images of them preparing a great vat of boiling fish, meat, fruit, and corn. Other images depict religious rituals. These customs fascinated Harriot, who emphasized the Algonquians' spiritual sensibilities in his text. For him, as for many other Europeans in the sixteenth century, the idea of expanding Christianity across the American continent was an urgent challenge for those who wanted to spread reformed Protestant practices. Harriot grasped that the English had a head start in Virginia. "Some religion they have alreadie," he wrote, "which although it be farre from the truth, yet being [as] it is, there is hope it may bee the easier and sooner reformed."[27]

Still, the Algonquians' spiritual universe operated differently from that of the English. "They beleeve that there are many Gods which they call Mantóac, but of different sortes and degrees," Harriot wrote, "one onely chiefe and great God, which hath bene from all eternitie." Harriot was incredulous when locals told him about two men who had recently died but afterward returned to their communities to warn the living about the dangers that lay ahead for those who did not live honorable lives.[28]

Harriot also dismissed the Algonquians' conception of the English. The locals had observed that there were no women among the newcomers and that the Europeans did not die of the diseases that arrived with them. They concluded that these uninvited visitors, as Harriot put it, "were not borne of women, and therefore not mortall, but that wee were men of an old generation many yeeres past then risen againe to immortalitie." The Algonquians also offered an explanation for their own mortality. They told Harriot that the English walking on the earth were accompanied by unseen others who shot "invisible bullets" into indigenous bodies. The English thought such explanations were nonsense. Harriot noted that local physicians "excuse[d] their ignorance" in curing the ill by convincing "the simple people" that "the strings of blood that they sucked out of sicke bodies, were the strings wherewithal the invisible bullets were

tied and cast."[29] Still, Harriot believed it crucial to detail Algonquian beliefs so that his readers would have "good hope they may be
brought through discreet dealing and government to the imbracing
of the trueth, and consequently to honour, obey, feare and love
us."[30] Harriot knew that the Algonquians were wrong about the
cause of the epidemics, citing the fact that there had been a solar
eclipse earlier that year and that a comet had appeared a few days
before the illness began to spread among the Natives—two signs the
English associated with ailments.[31]

Scholars routinely employ Harriot's text and the de Bry engravings together because they were linked in the 1590 edition. Yet this
method of interpretation elides the distinctions between the text,
composed by Harriot, and the captions, likely written or suggested
by Hakluyt.[32] Further, de Bry or those working with him selected
only some from White's original images for the printed version.
They left out, for example, White's pictures of Puerto Rico, where
the English ship had landed on its way to Carolina in 1585. Nor did
the engravers include a series of images of avian, terrestrial, and
aquatic flora and fauna that White had painted.[33] The omissions
had the effect of minimizing White's skills, particularly his ability to
depict *naturalia*, which he did (one could argue) with a more deft
hand than he possessed for depicting scenes of people.

Perhaps even more revealing, the engravers made substantial alterations in the images they chose to reproduce. In addition to in-
venting backgrounds for the individuals White had placed on otherwise blank pages, they also inserted details that did not exist in the
originals. The girl who appears with the "chief Ladye of Pomeiooc,"
for example, holds an Elizabethan doll in her hands in the original
painting. In the engraved version, she still holds the doll, but now
she waves an armillary sphere in one hand. Further, the brief caption
on the painting expanded to note how women and girls dressed,
explaining the Algonquians' custom of changing women's appear-

ance at important points of the female life cycle.[34] Other engravings reveal additional alterations from the watercolors. White had painted what he labeled "The Tombe of their Werounes or chiefe personages," which included the idol Kiwasa sitting next to the corpses on a raised platform with a fire smoldering unattended below. By contrast, the engraving has added a priest tending the flaming fire underneath and now the scaffolded tomb sits within a larger wooden building, likely the structure in the bottom left corner of the painting of Secota.[35]

The engravers also adjusted the depiction of American nature. White had labeled one image "The manner of their fishing" and used it to show eight men—four in a canoe in the foreground, two standing in shallow water with spears in their hands, and two more

FIGURES 35 AND 36 (*opposite*). While there is little doubt that the engravers in Frankfurt relied on White's paintings for details about the look of particular Algonquians he had met in 1585, the images differ. White's watercolor seems to be a preliminary sketch for a planned later work. The engraving represents one way to contextualize such an image—namely, by setting a figure in the foreground and creating a background for it. The backgrounds of the figures in the engravings in the *Brief and True Report* carried the same symbolic weight as the details to be found in a contemporary portrait. Whatever a viewer made of the un-European visage of the figure, the land contained an abundance of natural resources awaiting bold newcomers who could harvest them. Courtesy of the British Museum and the Huntington Library.

in a distant canoe demonstrating techniques for capturing fish and shellfish. It is an impressive picture of a people who know how to use paddles, nets, spears, and seines to haul what they want from the water. In the engraved version, four men still work from a canoe in the forefront, but the waters now contain much more aquatic life, including crabs, a turtle, an eel not evident in the painting, and many fish. In addition, many more people appeared: six are using spears to fish while six more canoes paddle in the background. The seine has evolved too. The painting featured a holding tank, presumably where caught fish remained until needed (similar to a modern lobster trap, at least in theory). But in the engraved version, that trap has evolved into four different devices of decreasing size that White never painted.[36]

The shift in media from original watercolor to published engraving had perhaps the greatest impact on the depiction of the town of

The manner of their fishing.

FIGURES 37 (*opposite*) AND 38 (*above*). Europeans, including the English, were often struck by Americans' command of aquatic resources, which ranged from Inuit ability to harvest walrus to pearl diving in the Caribbean. White's painting focused on what he quite likely saw with his own eyes. But in the hands of de Bry's engravers, the waters off the outer banks came to resemble proto-industrial aquatic farms, with more creatures to be harvested and better equipment for doing so. The engraver added numerous details without any visual clues from White's hand, a sign that the image could be manipulated to serve the larger political and economic ends of those responsible for the publication. Courtesy of the British Museum and the Huntington Library. (See Plate 10.)

Secota.[37] Although crafted by a European hand, White's painting provides the best access other than the archaeological record for understanding how Carolina Algonquians adapted to the local environment and shaped it to meet their needs. His painting depicted three fields, each with a different function. He labeled the field in the top right "Their rype corne," the one below "Their greene corne," and the lowest "Corne newly sprong." The Carolina Algonquians did not plant their crop at a single time, as the English would likely have done, but instead staggered their corn so that it would ripen in succession, presumably in order to produce several crops so they could consume fresh maize throughout the growing season and a surplus they could store for later use.[38] They also built a scaffold where one member of the community guarded the ripened corn from natural predators "for there are such number of fowles, and beasts," Harriot added, "that unless they keepe the better watche, they would soone devoure all their corne. For which cause the watcheman maketh continual cryes and noyse." The original painting also suggests that the Algonquians cleared more territory than de Bry was willing to depict: the trees are thinner, and no hunting occurs at the edge of the community.

White's image is also remarkable for what it lacks. There are no fences because the Algonquians had no need to keep penned livestock or to protect their fields from grazing animals. It was enough, as White's painting demonstrated, to station a lone man on a small scaffold to shout at ravenous birds and animals. The Algonquians did not lack knowledge of fences, as the depiction of the settlement at Poomiooc revealed. Presumably, if local animals had been as destructive or as numerous as hungry European livestock, the Algonquians would have erected fences to protect their crops at Secota.

The engraved version, produced by de Bry himself (as indicated by his initials on the bottom of the page), introduced a series of radical changes to White's vision of Secota. The left side of the picture included carefully planted sunflowers and tobacco, already popular among Europeans. The cornfields on the right of the picture no longer reveal serial planting spaced over months. Instead, the caption mentions only the need to space the plants a certain distance apart, for if planted too close together, "one stalke would choke the growthe of another and the corne would not come unto his rypeurs." The engraving also suggests that the Algonquians planted their maize in precise rows, thereby mimicking (on paper) the kind of distribution of plants that might be found in an English field or at least in contemporary agricultural manuals.[39] De Bry made other changes to the image that similarly imposed European sensibilities. In his version, the houses line up more strictly along the straight path running through the center of the image. He has also inserted access to a river (at the top of the page) where it logically must have existed and where, according to the caption, the Natives obtained their fresh water. White did not include that detail in his image of Secota, although his map of eastern North America from Chesapeake Bay to Florida did locate Secota near—if not quite on the banks of—a river.[40]

Each revision of the images by de Bry's workshop constituted a manipulation of the eyewitness visual information about coastal Carolina. The changes benefited those in England eager to promote the colonization of North America. That cause had gained impetus during the 1580s largely as a result of the partnership between Hakluyt and Sir Francis Walsingham, the queen's close advisor. The promoters were eager to establish a legal English claim to eastern North America by gaining possession that would not be challenged by the Algonquians or rival Europeans. But the visual evidence represented an imaginative colonial impulse as well. The promoters wanted to persuade Britons that this place was already primed for the newcomers. Indeed, the first captioned plate, which has no analog in the White paintings, depicted "The arrival of the Englishemen in Vir-

Within the image: *Their ripe corne.* · *Their greene corne.* · *Corne newly sprong.* · *Their sitting at meate* · *The place of solemne Prayer.* · *The house wherin the Tombe of their Herounds standeth.* · SECOTON· · *A Ceremony in their prayers wth strange testures and songs dansing abowt posts carued on the topps lyke mens faces.*

FIGURES 39 (*above*) AND 40 (*opposite*). The changes from White's watercolors to de Bry's engravings suggest how those responsible for the mass production of the picture recognized that this view could be the most effective at convincing European Protestants, especially in England, to settle what the English then called Virginia. Courtesy of the British Museum and the Huntington Library. (See Plate 11.)

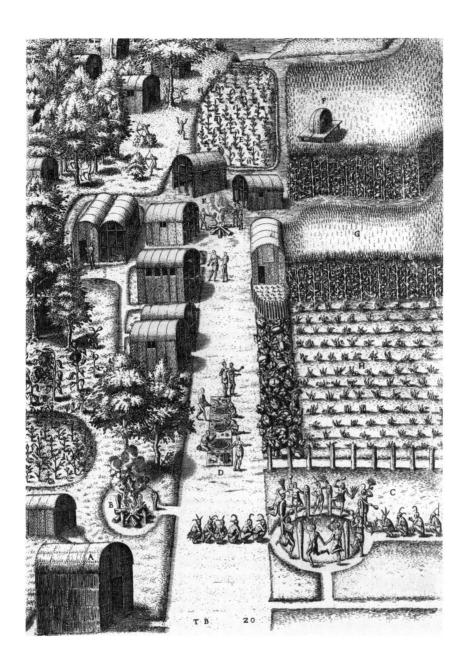

ginia." In the succeeding pages, the alterations from the watercolors to the engravings emphasized the promoters' message: if the Algonquians could live successfully in Virginia, such an argument ran, imagine what European Protestants could do in such a bounteous country? The engraved landscape became a new kind of claim to ownership, not of territory alone but its improvement through more suitable and sophisticated uses of nature.

The image of Secota, then, does not suggest a newfound Eden free of troubles, as some early English travelers to the region had proposed. Indeed, even de Bry's version of Eve handing Adam an apple, which appeared in the 1590 edition of Harriot's book along with pictures of Algonquians, reveals a transitional moment. The foreground depicts the end of the age of innocence, while small scenes in the background reveal the older Eve with a son and Adam tilling a field, representing the next stage of Christian history.[41] Instead of a static paradise, the picture of Secota summarized the Algonquians' attempts to organize and exploit a specific environment in a particular region of America. Their disinterest in domesticating livestock and their unwillingness to practice individual ownership of property confirmed European assumptions that Americans were not using the land as God intended. The Algonquians' ecological sensibilities hence became additional proof that North Americans' resources could be justifiably claimed by those who arrived with the Christian God's blessing and who shared His views about the environment.

Harriot's text holds the key to understanding the depictions of this landscape by White and de Bry. The *Briefe and True Report* revealed much about Algonquians' views of the natural world that did not appear in the images. Harriot was in some sense an ethnographer. He had learned how to communicate with the Carolina Algonquians through his work with Manteo and Wanchese, two Americans transported to England the previous year.[42] Relying on their expertise, Harriot came to learn much about how the Algonquians understood the world they inhabited, as well a the world of the spirits, which remained invisible to English eyes.

Harriot informed his readers that he had told the Algonquians about the Bible and had showed them a copy of the book. "I told them the booke materially & of it self was not of anie such virtue," he wrote, "as I thought they did conceive, but onely the doctrine therein co[n]tained." But members of his audience had reached out to grasp the object itself. They were "glad to touch it, to embrace it, to kisse it, to hold it to their brests and heades, and stroke over all their bodie with it; to shewe their hungrie desire of that knowledge which was spoken of." The Algonquians perhaps could be expected to abandon their heathen practices for Christianity after learning about the true religion. They saw the book as a talisman.[43]

Harriot also wrote about the Algonquians' belief in the immortality of the soul. He had heard about two possible destinations for the dead: some Algonquians traveled to what he called "the habitacle of gods" where they enjoyed "perpetuall blisse and happinesse"; the less virtuous fell into "a great pitte or hole," where they burned continuously. They called this latter destination "Popogusso." How, Harriot wondered, did they know about this place? "For the confirmation of this opinion, they tolde mee two stories of two men that had been lately dead and revived againe," he wrote, later noting that his informants were local priests. One of the events had taken place "but few yeres before our coming in the countrey of a wicked man which having beene dead and buried, the next day the earth of the grave beeing seene to move, was take[n] up again." He was on his way to Popogusso, he warned, when a benevolent deity intervened and brought him back to earth so that he could "teach his friends what they should doe to avoid that terrible place of torment." That same year, in a town sixty miles away, another dead man arose from his grave. According to Harriot's informants, he "shewed that although his bodie had lien dead in the grave, yet his soule was alive, and had travailed farre in a long broade waie, on both sides whereof grewe most delicate and pleasa[n]t trees, bearing more rare and excellent fruites then ever hee had seene before or was able to expresse." Soon the man claimed he came to a beautiful cluster of houses and met his father, who had died earlier. His father told the recently deceased man that he should return home to "shew his friendes what good they were to doe to enjoy the pleasures of that place," and after he did so he should come back again.

Harriot believed that these stories were fabrications employed by weroans and holy men, who spun such tales to "the common and simple sort of people that it maketh them have great respect" for these leaders. If Algonquians were going to avoid the horrors of Popogusso, they should not become "stealers, whoremoongers, and other sortes of wicked doers."[44] Harriot accepted the ethical precepts here. But the way that he phrased his brief description echoed one of the core ideas that Protestants had leveled against the Catholic Church since the early decades of the century. By bringing a bible to the Algonquians, Harriot was furthering the reform of Christianity by suggesting to putative neophytes that they did not need the intercession of specific individuals to understand holy writ. Harriot believed that the English had already made inroads among Americans. By "conversing with us," he wrote, "they were brought into great doubts of their owne, and no small admiratio[n] of ours." He claimed they wanted to learn still more, but the English did not yet have sufficient linguistic facility to convey more subtle and complex ideas.[45] Yet even that ignorance did not prevent progress, or so he thought. Harriot presumed that the conversations the English had with the Algonquians had initiated the colonization of the region by convincing the Natives that they could live alongside the newcomers and embrace a shared pursuit. By demonstrating that they were "true serva[n]ts" of the Christian God, the English told them that they "might live together with us, bee made partakers of his truth & serve him in righteosnes[s]."[46]

Yet while much of what Harriot wrote in the text found its way into either White's paintings or the de Bry workshop engravings, there is no visual record of the Algonquians' communication with the land of the souls. Instead, there are depictions of the idol called Kiwasa. There are no pictures of the invisible bullets, no attempt to render what an invisible Englishman might look like, no imaginary scene of Popogusso. They did not try to disguise the Algonquians' unchristian beliefs: the top of the title page of the 1590 edition shows both the conjurer and the priest adoring Kiwasa, who presides over the page (and even the book's title) just as surely as he presided over the tomb of the dead werowans in one of the book's engravings. But that was as far as it went. Pictures of the Algonquians' supernatural world would have revealed a different kind of landscape that remained in thrall to indigenous spirits. That was not the artists' point.

The 1590 edition of the *Briefe and True Report* immediately began to influence English attitudes regarding American colonization. The first three parts of the book consisted of Harriot's original text. Part one focused on "merchantable commodities." Part two was about "suche commodities as Virginia is knowne to yeelde for victual and sustenance of mans life, usually fed upon by the natural inhabitants: as also by us during the time of our abroad." The third part contained information that would be useful to any Englishmen who went to settle there, including "a description of the nature and manner of the people of the countrey." The fourth part, introduced by de Bry, consisted of a sequence of images of Carolina and its peoples. It began with the engraving of the Garden just before Eve hands Adam the forbidden fruit. The narrative sequence took the story from the arrival of the English through a series of portraits set into landscapes, followed by scenes of economic and religious activity, then by pictures of the palisaded community of Pomeiooc and the open town of Secota, and concluding finally with images of the idol Kiwasa, the ossuary of deceased weroans, and the tattoos common to particular settlements. The fifth part of the 1590 edition presented a series of images of Picts and other ancient inhabitants of Britain, purportedly based on an old chronicle and intended to show, as the caption read, "that the Inhabitants of the great Bretannie have been in times past as savage as those of Virginia."

From that moment on, Secota and the images of the Carolina Algonquians claimed a permanent position in English and other Europeans' history and visual culture. In 1610, Edmond Bolton engraved some of the tattoos in his study of heraldry, entitled *The Elements of Armories*, thus proving that the de Bry pictures had gained expanded meaning not necessarily related to colonization or American Natives per se. Bolton used the images to counter an argument made by government authorities that the peoples of the new world presented "the prime simplicity of our creation" and America a place as yet uncorrupted by "commerce." As Bolton pointed out, there were clear divisions among native peoples because the tattoos of Secota, Pomeiooc, and Aquasacock differed by locality.[47]

Three years later, Samuel Purchas, in the first version of his travel narratives, paraphrased much of the story about Secota and its peoples, emphasizing the religious issues that were the most revealing to him. "*They are great Wisards,*" he wrote. "Our artificiall Workes, Fire-workes, Gunnes, Writing, and such like, they esteemed the workes of Gods, rather then of Men, or at least taught vs by the Gods." He emphasized the significance of the idol Kiwasa: "They haue their Idoll in the inner-most roome of their house, of whom they tell incredible things. They carrie it with them when they goe to the Warres, and aske counsell thereof, as the Romans did of their Oracles. They sing songs as they march towards the battell, in stead of Drummes and Trumpets: their warres are bloudie, and haue wasted much of their people."[48]

What is more, although the English colonization of eastern North America effectively wiped out the Carolina Algonquians so that they vanished as distinct cultural groups, stories and pictures of Secota and nearby places remained. Captain John Smith drew on de Bry's engraving for the map he published in his *Generall Historie* of 1624. A half century later James Wooldridge drew on the same images in his oil painting of the indigenous peoples of Virginia.[49] In 1704, the printer of Robert Beverley's *History and Present State of Virginia* used new versions of selected images from the 1590 edition of Harriot's book to tell the history of the colony of Virginia—even though the places depicted in the scenes were not within the boundaries of the eighteenth-century province. Beverley's artist deviated from the de Bry engravings, especially in the depiction of Pomiooc, placing it near a cluster of houses outside the palisade. These Picts appeared again in 1720 when Henri Chatelain created an insert for a map of Britain.[50] Less than two decades later, the brilliant French engraver Bernard Picart also consulted the 1590 edition to create pictures for the survey of the world's religions that he produced with the scholar Claude Bernard. Neither Beverley nor Picart recreated the image of the town of Secota, but both drew on de Bry's versions of some of its inhabitants, including engravings of the women of the town, the idol Kiwasa, the religious men, and the ossuary of the deceased headmen.[51]

In the 1730s, Sir William Keith decided he would recount the history of early Virginia, tracing a story of initial optimism followed by tragedy. The explorers Amadas and Barlowe had been well treated and believed they had stumbled into Paradise, he informed his read-

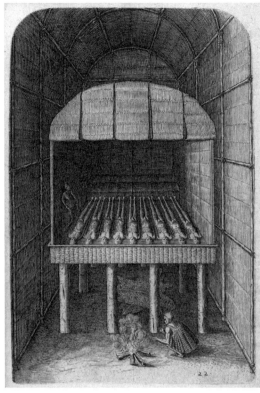

FIGURES 41, 42 (*above*), 43, AND 44 (*opposite*). The afterlife of the images from the de Bry engravings reveals the unusual staying power of this set of pictures. While authors of written reports would have known that they would be judged in comparison to other observers and would likely not find an audience for their work if they just recycled old tales, no new set of images challenged those produced by the de Bry workshop in 1590 until the nineteenth century, when the painter George Catlin's gallery of the native peoples of the American West offered new visions of indigenous peoples north of Mexico. The images here, from left to right, are from White's water-colors (from 1585), the de Bry edition of Harriot's *Briefe and True Report* (1590), Robert Beverley's history of Virginia (1705), and Bernard Picart's engravings for Claude Bernard's study of world religions (1741). Courtesy of the British Museum (Figure 41) and the Huntington Library (Figures 42–44).

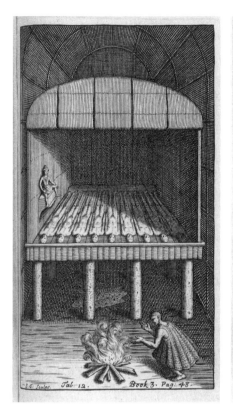

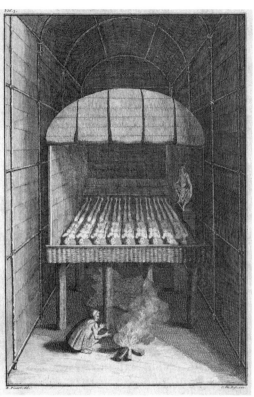

ers, but tensions soon set Algonquians and English against each other in cycles of murderous violence, culminating in the mysterious disappearance of the so-called Lost Colony—about a hundred English souls who vanished from coastal Carolina between the late summer of 1587 and the summer of 1589.[52] Writing at approximately the same time as Keith, William Oldys recounted a similar story in his biography of Sir Walter Ralegh, whose life had ended rather ignominiously and who was, in Oldys's opinion, robbed of the glorious reputation he deserved. Oldys emphasized the importance and accuracy of Harriot's account, which he supplemented with a manuscript that he claimed had been left in the Lambeth Library by Walsingham. While Oldys understood that events in Carolina eventually went badly, those developments occurred years after Ralegh first inspired the foundation of the colony as a bulwark against the noxious Spanish. Virginia, Oldys wrote, became a mission field for Protestants preaching true religion, a valuable new territory added to the queen's realm, and a place of employment for "the superfluous multitude of fruitless and idle people (here, at home, daily increasing) to travel, conquer, and manure another land."[53]

The original promise of this place was obvious, these later scholars recognized, in its name. After all, Ralegh did not name it after his virgin queen, they reminded their readers. Elizabeth had chosen the name, the historian William Stith wrote in 1753: the news of the "discovery was so welcome [in England], that the Queen herself was pleased to name the Country VIRGINIA, in Memory of it's having been first found out in the Reign of a Virgin Queen. Or as some have been pleased to gloss and interpret it, because it still seemed to retain the *Virgin* Purity and Plenty of the first Creation, and the People there primitive Innocency of Life and Manners."[54]

Stith further informed his readers of the central role that pictures had played in preserving the details of that formative encounter. He wrote that the queen had paid for the travel of John White, "a skilful and ingenious Painter," who crossed the Atlantic "to take the Situation of the Country, and to paint, from the Life, the Figures and Habits of the Natives, their Way of Living, and their several Fashions, Modes, and Superstitions; which he did with great Beauty and Exactness." Stith knew that White did not act alone. "There was one Theodore de Bry," Stith continued,

> who afterwards published, in the Year 1624, the beautiful Latin Edition of Voyages, in six Volumes, Folio, a most curious and valuable Work. He being in England soon after, by the Means of the Rev. Mr. Richard Hackluyt, then of Christ's Church, in Oxford, who, De Bry tells us, had himself seen the Country, obtained from Mr. With [White] a Sight of these Pieces, with Permission to take them off in Copper Plates. These, being very lively and well done, he carried [them] to Frankfort, on the Maine, where he published a noble Edition of them, with Latin Explanations, out of John Wechelius's Press, in the Year 1590. And these are the Originals from which Mr. Beverley's, and the Cuts of many of our late Writers and Travellers, have been chiefly imitated. And to shew, that the Inhabitants of England were once as wild and barbarous as these of Virginia, Mr. With gave him the Figures of three of the Picts, and two of their Neighbours, that he had found delineated in an old English History; which were accordingly published with them, and was no mean or impolitic Device, to recommend the Prosecution of the Enterprise to the English Nation.[55]

Stith's comments suggest one way to understand how later Anglo-Americans interpreted sixteenth-century Secota and the Carolina Algonquians. The next generations of scholars and writers, such as the American historian Jeremy Belknap at the end of the eighteenth century, repeated the story that explorers of 1584 had discovered a people "as 'gentle, loving, and faithful; void of guile and treachery; living after the manner of the golden age; caring only to feed themselves with such food as the soil affordeth, and to defend themselves from the cold in their short winter.'"[56] Things got worse later, Belknap acknowledged, but he believed in the peaceable origins of Virginia because he had ample proof that the story was true. The proof was, of course, the de Bry project, which expanded after the publication of Harriot's *Report*. "You ask if there is any book that pretends to give any account of the traditions of the Indians, or how one can acquire an idea of them?" Thomas Jefferson wrote to John Adams on June 11, 1812. He suggested that Adams try to find "the three folio volumes of Latin of De Bry," which contained "more original and authentic" material than some later commentators. But getting these books would not be easy. "This is a work of great curiosity, extremely rare, so as never to be bought in Europe, but on the breaking up, and selling some antient library," Jefferson added. That was how he obtained one for his library, which was "probably the only one in America."[57]

Secota, immortalized in text and image, was a place of great plenty, of people with a promising if primitive religion, and a beachhead in the battle against the spread of Catholicism. By the eighteenth century, the narrative had shifted to emphasize the Amadas and Barlowe version of an Edenic America based on the engravings of Secota and other Algonquian locales, which continued to influence the English colonial imagination. The circulation of these images was no accident. Other visual depictions of America had circulated among the crowd of promoters eager to establish an English presence in eastern North America in the late sixteenth and early seventeenth centuries. Those illustrations taught readers that the outer banks of Carolina were a far more inviting location for a colony than, say, the Arctic, which was depicted in multiple histories of Frobisher's expeditions of the 1570s as a forbidding place that imperiled Europeans just as much as other northern locales.[58] In both the Amadas/Barlowe version and the de Bry engravings, Carolina Algonquians posed little threat to the English who crossed the Atlantic. There were no signs of cannibals, who had appeared in earlier illustrated tales of exploration, or the monsters of the Orinoco described by travelers, including Ralegh himself.

Most of the images in the Harriot/de Bry volume of 1590 anticipated colonial triumph. When Robert Beverley wrote his history of Virginia at the time of the colony's first centennial, he included the 1590 images of Carolina Algonquians as illustrations. But he opted not to reprint one later engraving from the de Bry workshop—the image of the so-called massacre of 1622, which had been created in the de Bry workshop by the Flemish engraver's son-in-law, Matthais Merrian, in 1627. That debacle was a part of Virginia's history too, of course, but it sent a different, less confident message. The five parts of the 1590 edition, by contrast, formed a reassuring history of English success and predicted conversion of Algonquians to English ways, which was why the Picts appeared at the volume's end. The later use of the images from the 1590 edition and the earliest travel reports from Carolina reveal that subsequent observers saw the value in that original English conception of the Algonquians, even when they realized that tensions between Natives and newcomers had led to unfortunate violence.

In the early 1840s, one anonymous engraver created a new set of images based on de Bry's to illustrate a book entitled *Graphic Sketches from Old and Authentic Works*. The preface spoke of the need for these pictures. "A want has been long felt and acknowledged of a work, that may come within the means of every one, on the subject of the Manners, Habits, and Personal Appearance of the aborigines of our country, at the time of its discovery and settlement

FIGURES 45 (*opposite*) **AND 46** (*above*). Unlike the engravings of the outer banks of Carolina, the images of the Arctic that circulated in the sixteenth century revealed it as a forbidding place. Frobisher had taken three Inuit captive in 1578 and brought them back to England, where the queen hoped to meet them. They died soon after, but enterprising artists included pictures of their activities in illustrated editions of the English explorer Dionyse Settle's travel narrative of his journey to Nunavut with Frobisher. Living along the cragged shores of the North Atlantic and Baffin Bay was hard enough on its own, but chances for survival diminished because of the dangers posed by polar bears, here (above) seen devouring one of the unfortunate sailors who had accompanied the Dutch explorer Willem Barentsz on his failed effort to get through the Northeast Passage. Wikimedia Commons and alamy.com.

FIGURE 47. The actual settlement of Secota inhabited by Carolina Algonquians and observed by White and Harriot had long since faded into memory
when this mid-nineteenth-century view appeared in an antiquarian treatise
purporting to illustrate traditional native lives. From *Graphic Sketches from
Old and Authentic Works Illustrating the Costumes, Habits, and Character of
the Aborigines of America* (New York, 1841).

by the hardy adventurers that planted civilization on its shores, and began a new volume in the history of the world."[59] Among the images was a redrawn version of the de Bry rendering of Secota, now re-created in the service of a heroic national history.

White and de Bry could not have guessed that their images, buffeted with new captions to explain what Americans and American nature were like, would become fixed in the English understanding of their early colonial moment. Nor would they have imagined, although they might have been pleased, that their visions would also become those of European-born American historians of later centuries. The paintings act now as a *memento mori*—a picture of a haunted place whose inhabitants would soon succumb to the invisible bullets of European newcomers. Without knowing it, White had painted a people and a landscape at the end of one history and the start of another.

POSTSCRIPT

The Theater of Insects

In 1590, the English physician and naturalist Thomas Moffet (sometimes spelled in contemporaneous texts as Moufet or Muffet and in some modern renderings as Moffett) completed the most extensive entomological study yet created in the Atlantic basin.[1] Moffet wrote his book in Latin for other scholars in Europe or perhaps European colonists who lived abroad. In 1634, the book appeared as *Insectorum sive minimorum animalium theatrum* (roughly translated as *The Theatre of Insects or Small Animals*). Derived from close study of a wide range of authorities on nature, Moffet's treatise found enough of an audience to merit translation into English. In 1658, it appeared as an appendage to a massive work of natural history primarily devoted to mammals and fish. But it carried its own title: *The Theatre of Insects*. Like its Latin predecessor, it was filled with engravings, many of them set within the text as if insects had just landed on the page, inviting the reader to shoo them away. In its typography and layout, the book fit the title. Like an event on a stage, this was a spectacle, although one contained within bindings. But Moffet never saw how his English-reading audience responded to the show he offered. By the time the book appeared in English, he had been dead for over fifty years.

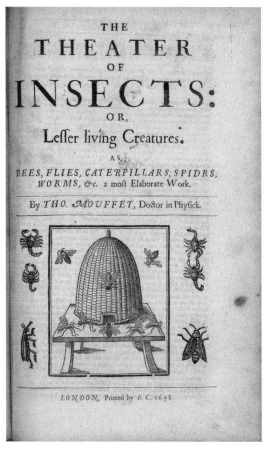

FIGURES 48 (*left*) AND 49 (*right*). Moffet's treatise, much of it drawn from earlier natural historians, had sufficient appeal in the seventeenth century that it appeared in Latin and almost a generation later in English. In addition to the labor needed to translate the text, there is considerable variation in the pictures in the books, as the title pages suggest. But despite the changes within, each title page presents bees and their hive, an illustration of the industriousness of the insect most important to sixteenth-century European commentators. Bees mattered because of the honey they produced, but they were also just as useful to humans as exemplars of virtuous behavior. Courtesy of the Huntington Library.

Moffet's *Theatre of Insects* was a monument to a particular kind of European scholarship at the end of the sixteenth century. It was not the most spectacular artistic rendering of natural elements by a European artist, a claim that might be made for Joris Hoefnagel's illustrations of the *Mira calligraphiae monumenta* (or *Model Book of Calligraphy*) for Emperor Rudolf II, which remain arguably among the finest illustrations of *naturalia*, both real and imaginary, known to exist. While Hoefnagel depicted more flowers than insects, his renderings of small moving creatures attest to the abilities of artists to illustrate insects with such a degree of scientific accuracy that modern observers can identify virtually all of them.[2] Moffet's more modest book distilled the lessons of others' works, primarily the unfinished opus of the Cambridge-based physician Thomas Penny, who had begun a major treatise on insects in the late 1560s but died in 1588 before it was completed. Moffet never claimed to be the sole author of his book. A 1598 title page linked him not only to Penny but also to Edward Wotton, who had published an important book on insects in 1552, and the Swiss scholar Conrad Gesner, who had produced a massive work of natural history earlier.[3] Moffet acknowledged the work of those who labored before him, a scholarly practice that was only emerging in the sixteenth century.[4] He wanted to bring the wisdom of recent scientific endeavors to the reading public, and that spirit of acknowledgment survived in the publication of his study of insects, for which the title page identified Wotton, Gesner, and Penny as those authorities on whom Moffet relied. That simple layout revealed a truth about the European understanding of the natural world in the sixteenth century: knowledge of nature was the product of collective long-term observation, which could be recorded and disseminated through the circulation of manuscript treatises or in printed books.

Europeans were not alone in their efforts to maintain a storehouse of knowledge about nature. From the late 1540s to the end of the 1560s, the Franciscan Bernardino de Sahagún worked with a series of Aztec informants to create what he called the *Historia general de las cosas de la Nueva España* or *General History of the Things of New Spain*. The book had multiple functions, among them transcribing the Aztecs' native Nahuatl so that Spanish scholars and colonial bureaucrats could learn it, as well as recording the history of the Aztecs and their conquest by Spaniards in the early sixteenth century. Sahagún's work also contained a natural history of Mexico, including information about indigenous insects. Understanding crucial aspects of Nahua culture would, Sahagún believed, enable the missionaries to advance the conversion of Americans and possibly help defend them against moral corruption by their sinful conquerors.[5]

Unlike Moffet's study, the *Historia general* did not provide the names of informants who had contributed to the natural history section. The work, like many European treatises about indigneous peoples in the Western Hemisphere, treated its subject in the ethnographic present, minimizing the ancient local knowledge of Natives to suggest they were living in a land that time had forgotten. Still, while Europeans could not access the accumulated wisdom that had been preserved in American media (such as Andean quipu and Mexican carved glyphs), the words spoken by Sahugún's informants and the images painted by the book's artists reflected the same careful observations about nature that Moffet also relied on. These artists, known as *tlacuilolli* according to the Nahuatl word for those who used paintings to record knowledge, adapted Renaissance representational strategies, thereby making their visual observations of nature more intelligible to European viewers. As one art historian recently argued, the images in this manuscript approximated "original indigenous voices" even when expressed in an adopted language. Of the almost 2,500 images in the manuscript, almost one-third—965 out of 2,486—depict the natural world. When the *tlacuilolli* painted with red made from cochineal, their art simultaneously depicted

American nature and promoted the use of an American product, which observers claimed reached well beyond Europe.[6] Nature was as grand a spectacle for Americans as it was for Europeans. Even insects, as it turns out, could be impresarios, proving that sometimes the littlest creatures could put on the greatest show.

Europeans and Americans alike were fascinated by the anatomical structure of insects as well as bug behavior. By the latter decades of the seventeenth century, the notion of insects providing keys to human society had taken hold, reaching its apogee for Europeans in Bernard Mandeville's *Fable of the Bees*, first published in London in 1714. The metaphors in that work fit well for Europeans looking to nature for models of human behavior in an age of economic and territorial expansion. Moffet's work, by contrast, reveals the link between the ideas generated in Antiquity and the age of wide-scale colonization in North America.[7]

When the English-language edition of Moffet's book appeared in print in 1658, its translator understood that part of the narrative's appeal lay in the performative talents of its subjects. Virtually all bees, he wrote in his dedication of the volume,[8] possessed stingers "full of revenging poison," except for the king, who lacked such weapons since the one who possesses "the supreme power, who can overthrow all when he will at pleasure," naturally possessed "an imbred gentleness, whence it is that Kings by their proper attribute are called Fathers and Pastors of the People." Gnats sounded their "trumpets," which they also used to penetrate the skins of animals in order to suck out their blood. Butterflies, using a delicate proboscis to gain nutrients, "extended large wings painted by natures artificial pencil, with paints [that] cannot be imitated" and "to which the very Rainbow is scarse comparable." Moffet waxed on at length about the grasshopper, which "in the heat of the Dog-daies importunately beats upon the ears of travellers, which are so framed, that their concave belly is made vaulted under the Diaphragm, over which is extended a cover of a thin and dry membrane, like to a Drum, which lets in the air by an oblique turning, which being beaten by the regular and successive motion of their wings, and stomach, coming in at a strait passage, and presently dilated, being against the rough-cast wals of the hollow place, and refracted, makes a sound."[9]

Early modern understanding of insects differs from modern conceptions of bugs. Moffet, for example, asserted that the rhinoceros was "of the kinde of great Beetles."[10] Still, although pre-Linnaean classification systems diverged from those that emerged centuries later, the European fascination with the potential of insects and the drive to understand them stemmed from an acute desire to understand the larger workings of nature and to use nature's lessons to explore cultural and historical questions. Moffet's translator, for example, urged readers to study fireflies. "You shall behold the internal fire of Glow-worms fastened to their tails," he wrote, "and the torches of the Indian Cocuia that shines in the night, and overcomes Cimmerian darkness."[11]

The lives of insects offered more than models for human behavior. Entomology offered insights into alchemy. If caterpillars could become butterflies, and "if Animals and Plants can be transmuted, why should that be denied to Metals?"[12] Insects taught political lessons: "the Monarchical government of Bees, the Democratical of Ants, and the œconomical providence of them both."[13] Nor could intelligent observers ignore the architecture of beehives, which Moffet declared framed "the cells in the combs of wax, mathematically to an exact Hexagon; in the hollow places of a Wasps nest; in the various chambers of the Ant-hill, and winding Manders: in the joyning together whereof he saw granaries, chambers, hospitals, places of burial, besides the innumerable endowments of these indefatigable creatures, their functions and labours, and he could not admire or praise them sufficiently, who had spent a long time in the contemplation of them, thinking it a work worth his pains, his whole life past being employed in this negligent and very idle business."[14] Moffet also alerted readers that just as insects could inform, they could also erase. Like plants in a field devastated by locusts and grasshoppers, books themselves could fall victim to tiny moths, "the greatest enemies to the Muses & their darlings . . . which with a greedy belly and iron teeth (though their bodies be very smal) prodigally waste and rend the lucubrations of whole ages."[15]

Moffet himself was even more pointed about why both ancient authorities, notably Aristotle and Pliny, and modern polymaths, such as the voracious intellectual Gesner, believed it crucial to study insects. (Moffet was fond of ancient analogies; he compared his labors working on his book to the ten years that the Greeks waited for Troy to fall.[16]) Yes, humans needed to understand bugs in order to extract the benefits of their labor (of honeybees and silkworms, for example), but people also had to know their pests in order to reduce the threats of insects such as grasshoppers and moths. The world of "lesser creatures" was vital precisely because of the lessons it conveyed about cultural values. Echoing Pliny, Moffet reasoned that ants taught about "prudence," bees provided lessons in "justice," and both revealed the benefits of "Temperance." A gnat, so tiny that humans could barely see it, could penetrate the skin of a lion as effectively as a sword. "A man hath need of steel to bore into oaks," Moffet wrote, "which the Wood-worm eats hollow with her teeth as the sound can testifie." He equated the worm's tunneling teeth to the engraving tools of the ancient Greek sculptor Polyclitus.[17]

Moffet realized that insects drew less attention than nature's more magnificent creatures. Italians and English might differ in many ways, but they shared a prejudice: it was more exciting to see a bear or a lion than a gnat. "If any man bring from far the wonderful Bittour, Elephant, Crocodile, there is no men but runs quickly to see that, because it is a new thing and unusual," Moffet complained, "and when they have leave to see them as much as they will, they only wonder at their greatness, colour, and such things as fall under the apprehension of their senses." Yet people just ignored "Hand-worms, Worms in Wine, Earwigs[,] Fleas; because they are obvious to all men, and very small, as if they were but the pastimes of lascivious and drunken Nature, and that had been sober only in making those huge and terrible beasts." Promoters understood the business of nature. They arranged for rhinoceroses and African lions to travel to London, where they displayed the animals to people who would "pay money for their places on the scaffold, to behold them brought upon the stage." Great mammals displayed nature's wonders easily, Moffet acknowledged, but there was just as much to admire among the insects.[18] They were small in size and seemingly weaker than any adversaries. But, he argued, a giant Goliath was no match for a smaller David, nor was a cluster of Spanish pilots able to win against "one small Drake."[19]

Insects needed to be studied because knowledge of these small creatures would improve human health. "Imitate if thou canst the Spiders curiosity, endure the sting of the Spider Phalangium, avoid the nastiness of Lice, take a Gnat out of thy throat, sleep when Fleas or Wiglice bite fiercely, keep thy trees safe from Caterpillars; drive away Weevils, Trees-worms, Vine-worms, and Timber-worms," Moffet wrote. "[W]herefore as God shews his power more in this more notable Artifice of Insects, so his great mercy is more apparent, because there is hardly any disease of the minde or body, but a remedy may be fetcht from this store-house to cure them both."[20] Even a creature as fear inspiring as a horse leech had multiple health benefits, including being a cure for "all the melancholique and mad people" who were healed when physicians applied leaches to their rectal hemorrhoids.[21] Insects revealed the wondrous powers and infinite potential of God, a point Moffet made obvious to his readers. In a section on glowworms primarily devoted to mocking humans

PLATE I. A section of the cloister ceiling at Fréjus. Photo by the author.
(See Figure 2.)

PLATE 2. Monks and exotic animals at Fréjus. Photo by the author.
(See Figure 3.)

·IIII·
A Q VI SE
ponela Cochinilla enlas
nueuas plantas passados
seis meses y mas que se
plantaron. Iasemi
lla se pone por marçoya
bril alos arboles biejos
que alos nueuos es bien
no ponersela hasta q̃
tengan mas hedad
De seismeses O

V N
ANO

PLATE 3. Cochineal in the "Florentine Codex." British Museum.

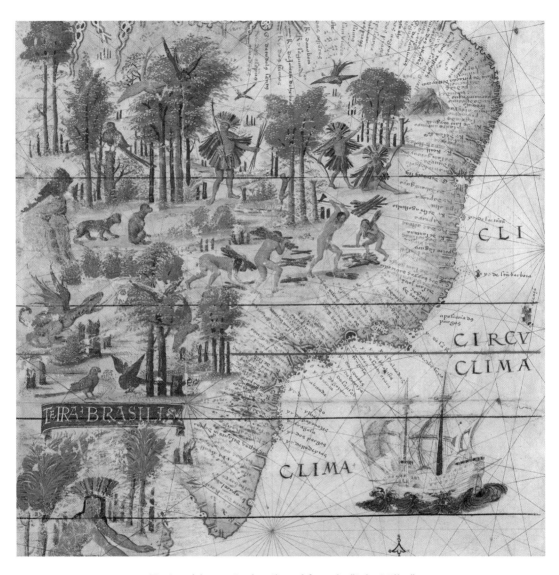

PLATE 4. Tupinambás carrying brazilwood from the "Atlas Miller." Bibliothèque Nationale. (See Figure 20.)

PLATE 5. Tupinambá headdress. National Museum of Copenhagen. (See Figure 21.)

PLATE 6. Brazil in the "Vallard Atlas." Huntington Library. (See Figure 14.)

PLATE 7. Pope in the "Vallard Atlas." Huntington Library. (See Figure 17.)

PLATE 8. Monsters in the "Vallard Atlas." Huntington Library. (See Figure 18.)

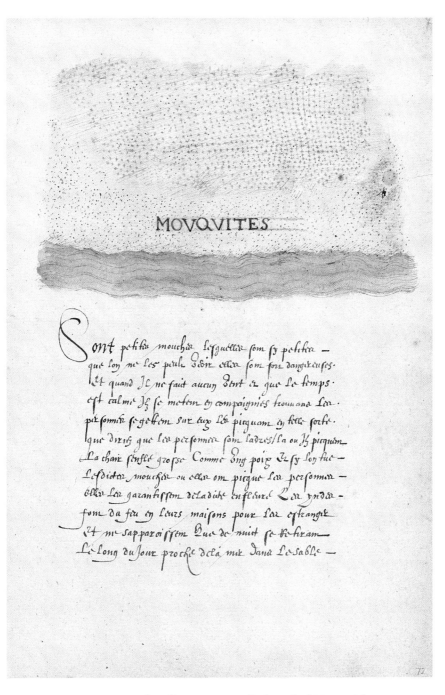

PLATE 9. Mosquitoes from "Histoire Naturelle des Indes." Morgan Library. (See Figure 31.)

The manner of their fishing.

PLATE 10. Fishing in Carolina according to John White. British Museum.
(See Figure 37.)

The ripe corne

Their greene corne.

Corne newly sprong.

Their sitting at meate

The place of solemne Prayer.

The howse wherein the Tombe of their Herounds standeth.

SECOTON.

A Ceremony in their prayers w.th strange testure and songs dansing abowt posts carued on the topps lyke mens faces.

7

PLATE II. Secota by John White. British Museum. (See Figure 39.)

PLATE 12. Firefly from "Histoire Naturelle des Indes." Morgan Library. (See Figure 50.)

who had tried to imitate their luminescence and failed, Moffet understood the genius of the brevity of the phenomenon. "For who is he that beholds the vanishing light of this, that doth not fix the eyes of his minde upon Christ the lasting, true, and the chiefest light of the world," he asked, "and doth not call to remembrance, that holy Spirit which doth illuminate our spirits in the most obscure darkness of our understandings?"[22] The lessons drawn from inquiry into tiny insect worlds had to be displayed like a play on a stage, hence the "theatre of insects."

Moffet's book contained 250 folio-sized pages crammed with text as well as scores of printed images. He began his investigations, perhaps not too surprisingly, with seven chapters on bee ecology, which included learned ruminations on the names of bees, their ethics and economy, their utility to humans, and the relationship between hives, drones, and thieving bees. Throughout, he described the property of bees in anthropomorphic language. Moffet thought of bees as "the principal" among all insects, which "are chiefly to be admired, being the only creature of that kinde, framed for the nourishment of Man." Other insects existed "to be useful in physic, or for delight of the eyes, the pleasure of the ears, or the compleating and ornament of the body," but "the Bee doth exceed them all in every one of these." No wonder that every major Western culture, from the ancient Hebrews to the modern Irish, had words for them, and many had laws as well.[23]

Bees were model denizens of the Earth whose behavior exhibited crucial instructive characteristics. Among other virtues, they modeled a good government. "Bees are swayed by soveraity, not tyranny," Moffet claimed, "neither do they admit of a King properly so called, by succession or by lot, but by due advice, and circumspect choice; and though they willingly submit to regall authority; yet so, as they retain their liberty, because they still keep their Prerogrative of Election; and when their King is once made sure to them by oath, they do in a principal manner love him."[24] Moffet, like earlier authorities, praised the "household vertues" of bees, which took care of their families and stored enough honey from the summer to have "a sufficient stock" to sustain them through the winter. They were clean in every way, never leaving excrement in their hives unless they were too ill to go outside; they only drank clean water; they did not kill enemies in their hives; and they disposed of the corpses of community members who died. Bees also possessed musical abilities, although not with the proficiency of elephants. They could not keep time when dancing, for example, but they could modulate the speed of flapping their wings to achieve a pleasing tune. They were even discrete in their breeding habits, always copulating out of sight of others inside their hives.[25]

Yet as bees mimicked the best human traits, so they were also subject to human failings. Hives could be wracked by civil strife, which could lead to outright wars between rival kings. (Moffet shifted his analysis when he wrote about wasps, referring to leaders of a hive as "masters" and adding that females governed during the winter; he also noted they were "governed by a Kingly power, not tyranny."[26]) When bees perceived that their hives were becoming overcrowded, the superior members eliminated some of the "common people." When roused by an external enemy, on the other hand, bees were as brave as any creatures to be found on God's earth.[27] "There is no creature under heaven so bold and adventurous as they are," Moffet declared, "insomuch, that whatsoever, whether man, or beast, or bird, or wasp shall molest them, vex and seek to destroy them, they sharply set themselves against, and according as they are able wound them with their stings."[28] In war, bees obeyed their superiors. They learned that parents had to be protective of young and that "youth or middle aged Bees" were to fetch whatever the king needed. They were tireless in their efforts to provide for the hive, even if it meant collapsing on the way home, unable to shoulder the load they felt compelled to bring.[29]

Bees' virtues fit a divine plan in which "God did create all creatures for our use," Moffet wrote, and "especially the Bees, not only that as mistresses they might hold forth to us a pattern of Politick and Oeconomick vertues, and inform our understanding; but that they might be able as extraordinary foretellers, to foreshew the success and event of things to come." Bees, he wrote, had swarmed four times shortly before the birth of Christ (in the years 90, 98, 113, and 208 BCE) and had also repeatedly shaped important political conflicts throughout human history. Bees featured prominently in works by Herodotus, Plutarch, Julius Caesar, and others. In book seven of Virgil's *Aeneid*, the arrival of a swarm warned locals that an invasion was imminent.[30] Wasps served as auguries too, according to Moffet, as in 190 BCE when "an infinite multitude of Wasps flew into the Market at *Capua*, and sate in the temple of *Mars*, they were with great diligence taken and burnt solemnly, yet they did foreshew the comming of an enemy, and the burning of the City."[31]

"What shall I say?" Moffet asked his readers. "God never created a creature less chargeable, and more profitable. They are bought for a very little money, they will live in all places whatsoever, even in woody and mountainous Countreys. The poor as well as the rich gain a great return or revenue by keeping of them, and yet need they not put more in the pot, or keep a servant the more for them." Keeping hives could produce sufficient honey to keep the economy of a small village afloat. Moffet concluded that humans could extract from their "shops or store-houses, Wax, Bee-bread, Bee-glew, Rosin, Honey-combs such as no Common wealth can be without."[32] Among the benefits were the health-giving properties of honey.[33]

Moffet's book was a landmark entomological study but hardly the last word.[34] Other scientists defined what it meant to be an insect: an arthropod with a body divided into segments, usually three pairs of legs, and antennae, and many of the over one million species have wings. The English naturalist Edward Topsell, whose writing on bees so closely paralleled Moffet's that he must have had the latter's manuscript in his hands when he wrote his *Historie of Serpents* (published in London in 1608), called insects "cut-wasted creatures."[35] Such a definition excluded many other animals commonly lumped together with insects, such as spiders and centipedes. Topsell included spiders and earthworms in his treatise, but he also had chapters on bees, hornets, wasps, and caterpillars, which fit the modern definition of insects, even if it seems odd that such descriptions could be found in a book on serpents.[36] But in earlier times, as the 1933 edition of the *Oxford English Dictionary* noted, the word "insect" had been more expansive and remained so "by the uneducated," who continued to lump together snails, worms, and even frogs with bugs. The English poet John Milton understood the common usage as well as anyone of his age when he wrote of Creation in *Paradise Lost* (vii: 476), "At once came forth whatever creeps the ground, Insect or Worme."

Moffet's rich text suggests the depth of his research about insects, but his book should not be confused with a modern work of entomology. Like many of his predecessors, Moffet looked to the insect world for behavior that echoed humans' antics. Study of the natural world helped people extract its benefits and avoid its costs but also yielded a different reward: nature was a mirror for humanity.

When American informants worked with Spanish missionaries to create codices describing precontact history and culture in modern Mexico and Central America, they too shared knowledge about bugs. This was nowhere more evident than in book 11 of Sahagún's

General History of the Things of New Spain. Like Moffet's treatise, this work detailed the physical structure of *naturalia* as well as the human uses of particular objects and creatures.

The information that Sahagún gathered from the Nahuas about insects was as precise as the details Moffet had learned in Europe. Locals explained that a caterpillar called *çacatecuilichtli* built cocoons only on cherry trees, yet their presence transformed the trees, which no longer bore any fruit.[37] A small locust, known as *tlalchapolin* or *ixpopoyochapolin*, was "stupid" because it delivered its young in the middle of a road and would not move even if they were about to be trampled.[38] Each species of ant needed its own description, but all shared a certain industriousness. An ant was "one which builds a nest for itself, builds a home for itself, makes an underground house for itself, hunts its food. It is a carrier, a transporter, a storer of things. It is a wood-dragger, a dragger of things." Some ants were venomous and bit people. The red ant (*tzicatana*) was known as "the conqueror" because it ate whatever it found. These creatures traveled in large masses so, the informants reported, "it is said they draw up for battle." Some ants got their names from where they could be found: the tree ant (*quauhazcatl*) and the dung ant (*cujtlaazcatl*). Most ants traveled in packs, but not the lone ant (*icel azcatl*), a "chili-red" insect only found on its own.[39] One ground-dwelling insect known as *tapaxi* or *tapayaxi* became known for its lascivious mating behavior.[40] The *tecuitlaololo* spent its time making balls out of dung and rolling them around, although sometimes pairs shared the burden. "It has," Sahagún reported, "no other particular function."[41]

Americans, like Europeans, studied the utility of bugs as well as their appearance and behavior. A centipede called *conyayaual* drew itself into a circle when threatened. Humans captured it and crushed it into a salve to spread on a painful tooth or inflammation caused by gout, but users needed to be wary since drinking a concoction made from *conyayaual* could be fatal.[42] Insects provided models for human behavior too, although they were not always as positive as the industrious ant. The *nextecuilin* tended to travel lying on its back, so, as the informants reported, "one who is not discreet is called *nextecuilin*: because he does not live as everyone [else] lives."[43]

Sahagún reported that marvelous insects could be found in Mexico. Among them was the *icpitl* or firefly. Four varieties could be found there, including a glowing butterfly, a glowing worm, and what the informants called a "butterfly-ant." The *coquitl* resembled a long locust and came out at night when it rained. Its light was so large that it took up half the length of its body. "Sometimes it shines like a pine torch, because of the dark," the informants reported. "And sometimes they just form a line as they travel along. And the uninformed name them *tlauipochtin*"—or sorcerers.[44] Luminescence attracted admiration, but so did other attributes of many small animals. None could match the potential of the cochineal, a kind of worm that grew on the leaves of the *nopal*, a tree that produced an edible fruit known as *tuna*. When consumed by pregnant women, it caused a fetus to move in the womb and so prevented breach birth. At the end of its life, cochineal became so engorged with fat that they looked like blood blisters on the leaves. Then they would fall off, and locals would sweep them up and then use them to produce a vivid red dye. Dead cochineal deemed inferior could be made into cakes and consumed.[45] Europeans quickly learned how to extract the dye as well, and saw cochineal as one possible solution for their seemingly insatiable demand for red coloring.[46] The insect and its uses soon found a place in the writings of natural historians of New Spain.[47]

Little about the observable world and its uses escaped the attention of Sahagún's informants. The chapter that described cochineal also included details about how the Mexica extracted other dyestuffs

from various natural resources to create the vivid colors that impressed European observers. Fine yellow (*xochipalli*) came from the *xochitl* flower and a light yellow (*çacatlaxcalli*) from a grass (*çacatl*) that resembled a tortilla—"wide, round, big, thin." The latter could be found in hot climates and was known for the intensity of its color. Blue came from the blossom of an herb. A chili-red dye could be made from the wood of the *uitzquauitl*, and a black dye, useful for writing as well as dyeing textiles, came from the *nacazcolotl*. Black could also come from the ash of pine pitchwood. Red ochre could be made from a rock known as *tepetate*. To get dark green, one needed to make a dye from the *yauhtli* (wormwood) tree; brown necessitated mixing cochineal and alum; brazilwood mixed with copperas produced a brown so deep it could appear black.[48]

In the process of learning about each other, the peoples of the Atlantic basin also studied the natural world around them. Individuals on both sides of the ocean came to realize the complex biodiversity of early modern environments. The French Huguenot Jean de Léry's narrative of his trip to Brazil, first published in Geneva in 1578, contained detailed information about American nature, including specific insects that either differed from species known to Europeans (bees) as well as minute pests known locally as *aravers, ton, yetin*, and *nigua*, which burrowed into human flesh and caused excruciating pain and even death. Newcomers who he knew would confront these vermin would do well to listen to what Americans did to minimize their threat.[49] Within fifteen years of its initial publication, Léry's study appeared in multiple languages, including illustrated German and Latin editions (although, unfortunately, the engravers did not include any depictions of the tiny tormenters the missionary had described). The conveyance of information, which began with firsthand observation from Native informants and became a written text and finally an illustrated book, facilitated the spread of information about American nature well beyond the land of the Tupinambás.

Léry's book, appearing near the end of the century, revealed how quickly Americans' information about the nature of the Western Hemisphere could circulate among Europeans. Sahagún's work did not appear in a printed version until the early nineteenth century, so it is unclear how far the details of his interpretation of nature traveled. Moffet, by contrast, set about his task at the end of a century of intellectual discovery for Europeans, a period so successful that he could integrate materials about American fireflies without paying much attention to the novelty of this information. In his hands, American observations of nature fit side by side with those of the ancients. The natural world of the Atlantic, in his mind, was an integrated whole.

The Columbian Exchange had altered life for millions, often un-leashing unseen forces as deadly as the microbes that felled so many Carolina Algonquians. Numinous powers remained, as they would for centuries in some communities, shaping the natural world and its human occupants. At the century's end, the light of fireflies of-fered partial illumination of the dark realms of the night and the creatures, worldly and otherwise, which roamed imaginations across a basin thrust into modernity.

L

NOTE ON SOURCES

"The attention of a traveller, should be particularly turned, in the first place, to the various works of Nature," the Anglo-American naturalist William Bartram wrote near the end of the eighteenth century, "to mark the distinctions of the climates he may explore, and to offer such useful observations on the different productions as may occur."[1] Along the western shores of the Atlantic basin, everyone was a traveler in the sixteenth century—a journeyer who crossed an ocean; another who followed game in winter and fish runs in the spring; a trader eager to obtain desirable lumber, mineral, or furs; a healer who needed to find *materia medica* to salve the wounds of a body or a soul; or a mapmaker who would record observations about nature on paper or inscribe details in his or her memory. All watched and learned. Everyone saw the alterations of landscapes and communities when Europeans met Americans, and the transmission of Western Hemisphere biota eastward across the Atlantic eventually altered European landscapes as well when farmers and gardeners planted potatoes, maize, tomatoes, and tobacco. American landscapes changed too, with the arrival of European ungulates and African rice.

But there was no single transformation from a precontact arena of stability to a postcontact sense of order. Humans changed nature frequently, as Timothy Dwight, a one-time president of Yale, understood. "A country, changing as rapidly as New-England," he wrote in his posthumously published narrative of travels printed in 1821, "must, if truly exhibited, be described in a manner, resembling that, in which a painter would depict a cloud. The form, and colours, of the moment must be seized; or the picture will be erroneous."[2] Americans and Europeans modified environments when they used fire to chase game, cleared forests by girdling trees to kill them, and chopped down tall straight trees to be used as masts on oceangoing ships. Humans altered the beds of streams and the Atlantic itself in their pursuit of gain. Africans drew on age-old knowledge about rice cultivation and did it so quickly in Brazil that some later scholars thought the crop must have been in the Americas before 1492. People also bore witness to the natural world—in their letters, in the stories they told each other, in the paintings and carvings they put in sacred spots.

The chapters in this book focus not on broad environmental change but instead on specific relationships between nature and culture, primarily in the sixteenth-century Atlantic basin. As these disparate situations reveal, there was not a single moment of transition but instead myriad encounters, which unfolded one after another after 1492, at times between the realms of the unseen and the quotidian. This book outlines sequential stages of the environmental history of the basin, or an arc of how humans understood nature at a time of extensive discovery.[3] What follows here are notes on the sources that I found most useful to understand the relationship between nature and culture in the sixteenth-century Atlantic basin.[4]

With rare exceptions—such as the eruption of a long-dormant volcano or a powerful earthquake that might also produce a tsunami—the natural world changes slowly. Species evolve, but alterations tend to be the result of random mutations that, over time, make some members better adapted to a particular place than others. By definition, evolution is a long-term and slow-moving process. Humans, however, can quicken the pace of environmental change. Ancient peoples burned forests and constructed irrigation ditches, each with long-lasting environmental consequences. They also transported animals and plants into new places. Yet while humans have been adapting their environments for millennia, the rate of change accelerated after 1492. Over the course of the following century, more people traveled longer distances than at any previous time in recorded history. There had been long-distance migrations earlier, of course, most notably the peopling of the Americas by the descendants of those who crossed the Bering Sea over a land bridge approximately 12,000 years ago, as well as the Polynesian peopling of the islands of the South Pacific, including modern New Zealand, the last place on earth settled by humans. But the frequency and range of migration that began with Columbus's voyages initiated a series of environmental changes on a previously unimaginable scale.

A generation ago, the environmental historian Alfred W. Crosby Jr. redefined our understanding of the relationship between the Americas and the Old World in *The Columbian Exchange: Biological Consequences of 1492* (Greenwood, Conn., 1492). In the years that followed, numerous historians, including some of the most artful and articulate, have traced complex long-term relationships between culture and nature. Anyone interested in pursuing the intellectual and cultural history of nature should begin with three luminous books: Keith Thomas, *Man the Natural World: A History of the Modern Sensibility* (New York, 1983); Simon Schama, *Landscape and Memory* (New York, 1995); and Donald Worster's field-defining *Nature's Economy: A History of Ecological Ideas* (orig. pub. 1977; 2nd ed., New York, 1985). These are works that are far more than interpretations of attitudes toward nonhuman nature. They constitute historical writing at its best.

Communities across the Atlantic basin needed to come to terms with the shifting environments they inhabited. They required new vocabularies to describe phenomena and material objects that they had never seen before, an adaptation elegantly described by John Elliott in *The Old World and the New* (Cambridge, Eng., 1969). Such vocabularies were not confined to the written or spoken word. Individuals also used their artistic training and talents to depict the new environment in visual images. The task was difficult in part because many artists never saw the places they tried to sketch or paint. They conjured entire visual worlds from verbal descriptions, often fanciful, produced by travelers. But these authors had quite possibly embellished their works to appeal to patrons, thereby reminding us of the difficulty of separating fact from fable, a point investigated in Percy G. Adams, *Travelers and Travel Liars, 1660–1800* (Berkeley, Calif., 1962).

Yet however inaccurate verbal, written, or visual depictions might seem, evidence from across the basin suggests the emergence of new environments across the Atlantic basin, as well as new concepts of ecology to explain them. These changes can be discerned at the microscopic level in the spread of infectious diseases, which had immediate consequences for victims and for the lands they once possessed. This phenomenon has attracted sustained attention by historians, including Alfred Crosby (see especially *Ecological Imperialism: The Biological Expansion of Europe, 900–1900* [Cambridge, Eng., 1986]) and David Jones (see "Virgin Soils Reconsidered," *William and Mary Quarterly* [hereafter *WMQ*] 3rd ser., 60 (2003), 703–742). Change also took place at the ground level, notably in the increase in the range of territory compacted by animal hooves, which either caused or accelerated the rate of erosion in specific locales. The movement of animals had a direct impact on local places, both where humans kept them and on lands, notably islands, where pigs (in particular), cows, and sheep spread on their own once humans left them there. Humans also pushed certain species away, at times to the point of extinction, with often devastating consequences for local populations, Native and newcomer alike. On these topics, see, among many sources, William Cronon, *Changes in the Land: Indians, Colonists, and the Ecology of New England* (New York, 1983); Elinor G. K. Melville, *A Plague of Sheep: Environmental Consequences of the Conquest of Mexico* (Cambridge, Eng., 1994); Timothy Silver, *A New Face on the Countryside: Indians, Colonists, and Slaves in South Atlantic Forests* (Cambridge, Eng., 1990); Virginia DeJohn Anderson, *Creatures of Empire: How Domestic Animals Transformed Early America* (New York, 2004); James D. Rice, *Nature and History in the Potomac Country: From Hunter-Gatherers to the Age of Jefferson* (Baltimore, 2009); and John Coleman, *Vicious: Wolves and Men in America* (New Haven, Conn., 2006). The pace of deforestation, already evident across much of Europe to support fuel and building needs, increased with the movement of trees useful for dyeing, although as Michael Williams has noted, for North America, substantial forest clearing took place after the sixteenth century (see his *Americans and Their Forests: A Historical Geography* [Cambridge, Eng., 1989]). For the European context, see Andrew McRae, "Tree-Felling in Early Modern England: Michael Drayton's Environmentalism," *Review of English Studies*, n.s. 63 (2011), 410–430; P. Warde, "Fear of Wood Shortage and the Reality of the Woodland in Europe, c. 1450–1850," *History Workshop Journal* 62 (2006), 28–57; and Karl Appuhn, *A Forest on the Sea: Environmental Expertise in Renaissance Venice* (Baltimore, 2009). For how fears of such shortages influenced the English in North America, see Keith Pluymers, "Atlantic Iron: The Political Ecology of Early English Expansion," *WMQ* 3rd ser., 73 (2016), 389–426. Fish populations came under increasing stress as well, especially the vast schools of cod off the northeastern shores of North America, which had been fished by Europeans since the Norse arrived at the turn of the millennium. The best work on this subject is W. Jeffrey Bolster's *The Mortal Sea: Fishing the Atlantic in the Age of Sail* (Cambridge, Mass., 2012). For the longer history of European uses of rivers and the ways that human communities adapted them to meet their economic needs, see Richard C. Hoffmann, "Economic Development and Aquatic Ecosystems in Medieval Europe," *American Historical Review* 101 (1996), 631–669.

These changes, all initiated by humans, drew the attention of writers and artists who described this emerging ecology, especially in the Western Hemisphere. The words and images that survive bear witness to both changes in the physical world and the psychological struggles of those trying to comprehend them. Here it is worth considering the literature on how Europeans made sense of American plants, the subject of such excellent work as Daniela Bleichmar, *Visible Empire: Botanical Expeditions and Visual Culture in the Hispanic Enlightenment* (Chicago, 2012) and Londa L. Schiebinger, *Plants and Empire: Colonial Bioprospecting in the Atlantic World* (Cambridge, Mass., 2004). Europeans also offered multiple studies of how climate worked, at home and in places where they colonized, as Anya Zilberstein reveals in *A Temperate Empire: Making Climate Change in Early America* (New York, 2016). Kim Todd's *Chrysalis: Maria Sibylla Merian and the Secrets of Metamorphosis* (New York, 2007) elegantly examines European fascination with insect life in the seventeenth-century Atlantic basin, especially in Suriname.

By the middle of the sixteenth century, even before the age of large-scale transportation of biota, images of useful American plants were circulating across Europe, adorning illustrated manuscripts and printed books alike, either as botanical specimens exhibited for study on an otherwise blank page or in helpful depictions of their use, with texts extolling a plant's particular virtues. Consider, for example, three American plants that quickly attracted the attention of Europeans: pineapple, maize, and tobacco. The first European image of a pineapple appeared in Gonzalo Fernández de Oviedo y Valdés, "Historia general y natural de las Indias" (HM 177, f. 46r, Huntington Library [hereafter HEH]), which then appeared in Oviedo, *La historia general de las Indias* (Seville, 1535), f. 76v and subsequently in [Oviedo], *L'histoire naturelle et generalle des Indes, isles, et terre ferme de la grand mer oceane*, trans. Jean Poleur (Paris, 1556), f. 110v; Giovanni Batista Ramusio, *Navigationi et Viaggi*, 3 vols. (Venice 1556–1559), III: f. 136r; and, later, [Caspar Plautius(?)], *Nova typis transacta navigatio: Novi orbis Indiæ occidentalis* (np, 1621), opp. 53. Similarly, maize first appeared in a European work in Ramusio, *Navigationi et Viaggi*, III: 131v. Tobacco became widely known through such works as Nicolás Monardes, *Primera y segunda y tercera partes de la historia medicinal de las cosas que se traen de nuestres Indias Occidentales que sirven en medicina* (Seville, 1574), f. [40r] (image) and 41r–50v (description of tobacco's benefits), and its English-language translation by John Frampton as *Joyfull Newes out of the Newfound World* (London, 1580). Almost simultaneously, these plants began to appear in works of cosmography as well as travel narratives or illustrated versions of reports from the field, which were subsequently disseminated by scholars such as the French royal cosmographer André Thevet and the Frankfurt-based Flemish engraver Theodor de Bry, for whom maize was central in his edition of Harriot's *Briefe and True Report of the New Found Land of Virginia* (Frankfurt-am-Main, 1590). For how the process worked for Monardes, see Daniela Bleichmar, "Books, Bodies, and Fields: Sixteenth-Century Transatlantic Encounters with New World *Materia Medica*," in Londa Schiebinger and Claudia Swan, eds., *Colonial Botany: Science, Commerce, and Politics in the Early Modern World* (Philadelphia, 2005), 84–99; for maize, the best work remains Betty Fussell, *The Story of Corn* (New York, 1992).

European travelers' encounters with the Americas expanded the Western understanding of nature, as became evident in the sixteenth century when novel flora and fauna began to appear with increasing

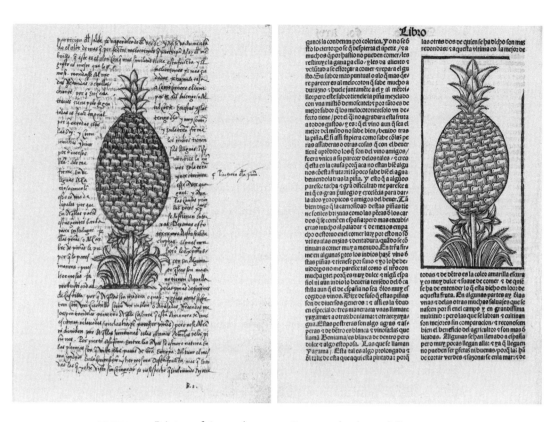

FIGURE 51. Printers of sixteenth-century European books used divergent strategies when publishing images of American flora. Hence the publisher of Fernando Gonzalez Oviedo y Valdes's *Historia General* mimicked the strategy of Oviedo's manuscript illustration and depicted a pineapple floating within a text. Courtesy of the Huntington Library.

regularity in European manuscripts and books; on this point, see Henry Lowood, "The New World and the European Catalog of Nature," in Karen Ordahl Kupperman, ed., *America in European Consciousness, 1493–1750* (Chapel Hill, N.C., 1995), 295–323. The art historian Amy Buono has explored how two kinds of *naturalia*, feathers and brazilwood, linked the worlds of Tupinambás and Europeans; see Buono, "Representing the Tupinambá and the Brazilwood Trade in Sixteenth-Century Rouen," in Regina R. Félix and

Scott D. Juall, eds., *Cultural Exchanges Between Brazil and France* (West Lafayette, Ind., 2016), 19–34, and "'Their Treasures Are the Feathers of Birds': Tupinambá Featherwork and the Image of America," in Alessandra Russo, Gerhard Wolf, and Diana Fane, eds., *Images Take Flight: Feather Art in Mexico and Europe, 1400–1700* (Florence and Mexico City, 2015), 178–189. The extraordinary vibrancy of materials from this era can be seen in two exquisite volumes edited by Jay A. Levenson: *Circa 1492: Art in the Age of Exploration* (Washington, D.C. and New Haven, 1991) and *Encompassing the Globe: Portugal and the World in the 16th and 17th Centuries* (Washington, D.C., 2007).

Ecological change did not begin in the sixteenth century, nor did awareness of aspects of environmental decline such as species extinctions and deforestation emerge only with the modern environmental movement. (For a superb study of the origins of contemporary environmentalism, see Adam Rome, *The Genius of Earth Day: How a 1970 Teach-in Unexpectedly Made the First Green Generation* [New York, 2013].) John Brooke's masterful *Climate Change and the Course of Global History: A Rough Journey* (New York, 2014) situates the early modern era within a vast timeframe yet remains sensitive to the particular developments of the post-1492 world with its intensification and expansion of long-distance trade and travel. As his study and others show, observing nature, as Bartram understood it at the end of the eighteenth century, was not a new phenomenon in the early modern era. Gaius Plinius Secundus, known as Pliny the Elder, was born in 23 CE and died when he went to get a closer look at the eruption of Mount Vesuvius in 79 CE. During his relatively brief life, he filled the pages of the thirty-seven volumes of his *Natural History* with details about the world known to ancient Mediterranean peoples—including news that he gathered from travelers who had gone abroad. (The entire set, translated by H. Rackham et al., was published in English in ten volumes by the Loeb Library of Harvard

University Press from 1942 to 1962.) The impulse to describe nature survived for centuries. Commentators as diverse as Zahiruddin Muhammed Babur (the founder of the Mughal Empire), the mid-thirteenth-century to early fourteenth-century Venetian traveler Marco Polo, and the fifteenth-century Chinese chronicler Ma Huan all described places they observed, often focusing on what struck them as inferior to their homelands or what seemed outlandish. The narrative of the English knight John Mandeville, spiked with fantastic and imaginary observations of a mythical "East," transfixed Europeans and spread across the continent long before the printing press made the circulation of texts easier. Seen from this longer historical perspective, surviving sources that describe nature in the sixteenth-century Atlantic basin might seem to be little more than a continuation of a seemingly innate human desire to talk or write about new places. Fortunately, these sources can be found in accessible modern English editions. See Babur, *The Baburnama*, trans. Wheeler M. Thackston (New York, 1996); Ma Huan, *Ying-Yai Sheng-lan: The Overall Survey of the Ocean's Shores* [1433], trans. J. V. G. Mills, Hakluyt Society Extra Series no. 42 (Cambridge, Eng., 1970); *The Travels of Marco Polo*, trans. Ronald Latham (Harmondsworth, Eng., 1958); and *The Travels of John Mandeville*, trans. C. W. R. D. Mosely (London, 1983). These narratives include much more than observations about nature, of course, and need to be understood as travel accounts, a genre that has attracted intense and excellent commentary by scholars such as Mary Blaine Campbell (*The Witness and the Other World: Exotic European Travel Writing, 400–1600* [Ithaca, N.Y., 1988]), Mary Fuller (*Voyages in Print: English Travel to America, 1576–1624* [Cambridge, Eng., 1995]), Joan-Pau Rubiés (*Travel and Ethnology in the Renaissance: South India Through European Eyes, 1250–1625* [Cambridge, Eng., 2000]), and Muzaffar Alam and Sanjay Subrahmanyam (*Indo-Persian Travels in the Age of Discoveries, 1400–1800* [Cambridge, Eng., 2007]). By the time painters decorated the cloister at Fréjus in the fourteenth century, images of the monstrous and the fantastic could be found in bestiaries and in church sculpture; see Susan Crane, *Animal Encounters: Contacts and Concepts in Medieval Britain* (Philadelphia, 2013); the beautifully illustrated work by Michel Pastoureau, *Bestiaires du Moyen Âge* (Paris, 2011); and Kirk Ambrose, *The Marvellous and the Monstrous in the Sculpture of Twelfth-Century Europe* (Woodbridge, Suffolk, 2013).

Such sources provide ample evidence for modern historians eager to explore the relationship between human societies and physical environments. Among the earlier scholars of changes in the environment was George Perkins Marsh, an intrepid philologist appointed by President Abraham Lincoln to be the ambassador to Italy in the early months of the Civil War. Marsh remained in Rome until his death in 1882, but today he is best known as the author of *Man and Nature; or, Physical Geography as Modified by Human Action*, which was published originally in New York in 1864. The book was a monument of historical imagination appearing amid the worst cataclysm the United States has ever suffered. Marsh's concern was the long history of human habitation of the Earth, which had produced catastrophic consequences. "The destruction of the woods," he wrote, "was man's first physical conquest, his first violation of the harmonies of inanimate nature." Marsh added that people then extended "over the unstable waters the empire" that they "had already founded upon the solid land." Humans, he argued, had forgotten that they had the Earth "for usufruct alone, not for consumption, still less for profligate waste." Marsh's text became widely available in a phenomenal modern edition by David Lowenthal, published in 1965, and was reissued in 2003 with a foreword by William Cronon by the University of Washington Press.[5]

Over the course of the twentieth (and into the twenty-first) century, a number of scholars have identified and analyzed attitudes toward nature that have direct relevance for those who seek to understand ecological change in the sixteenth-century Atlantic basin. Two excellent studies that analyze prevailing sentiments in the Old World before 1492 are Clarence J. Glacken, *Traces on the Rhodian Shore: Nature and Culture in Western Thought from Ancient Times to the End of the Eighteenth Century* (Berkeley, Calif., 1967), which carefully explicates Western (that is, Mediterranean and European) views of the natural world from antiquity through the eighteenth century, and James S. Romm, *The Edges of the Earth in Ancient Thought* (Princeton, N.J., 1992), which focuses on writers such as Pliny and their views of the world beyond their local horizons. Emilio Sereni's *History of the Italian Agricultural Landscape* (which appeared originally as *Storia del paesaggio agrario italiano* in 1961 and was subsequently translated by R. Burr Litchfield [Princeton, N.J., 1997]) traces two millennia of environmental change while Mauro Ambrosoli's *The Wild and the Sown: Botany and Agriculture in Western Europe, 1350–1850*, trans. Mary M. Salvatorelli (Cambridge, Eng., 1997) stands as an exhaustive account of attitudes and practices of medieval to modern Europeans. The scholarly literature becomes more abundant for the period after 1500. James Raven's *English Naturalists from Neckam to Ray: A Study of the Making of the Modern World* (Cambridge, Eng., 1947) remains a monument of a certain kind of close historical reading that pivots on almost microscopic analysis of texts and elucidates links between earlier writers. The entomologist Steve Nicholls's *Paradise Found: Nature in America at the Time of Discovery* (Chicago, 2009) presents an astonishing survey of the richness of early American environments before the spread of the modern industrial economy, which is in some ways a new account of the subject treated earlier in John Bakeless's classic work, *America as Seen by Its First Explorers: The Eyes of Discovery* (Philadelphia, 1950). Stuart B. Schwartz's *Sea of Storms: A History of Hurricanes in the Greater Caribbean from Columbus to Katrina* (Princeton, N.J., 2015) is a sobering account of the difficulty of transatlantic travel well before our age of increasing climate instability and a reminder that sailing ships faced troubles in warm waters just as they did in the north, a subject I explored in *Fatal Journey: The Final Expedition of Henry Hudson—A Tale of Mutiny and Murder in the Arctic* (New York, 2009).

Fortunately, many sixteenth-century texts, including travel narratives that present details about the environments European explorers saw and conversations visitors had with Americans, are now available in modern editions. See, for example, José de Acosta, *Natural and Moral History of the Indies*, trans. Frances López-Morillas and ed. Jane E. Mangan (orig. pub. 1590; Durham, N.C., 2002); Thomas Harriot, *A Briefe and True Report of the New Found Land of Virginia* (orig. pub. Frankfurt-am-Main, 1590; facsimile rpt. New York, 1972); and Jean de Léry, *History of a Voyage to the Land of Brazil*, trans. Janet Whatley (orig. pub. Geneva, 1578; Berkeley, Calif., 1990). Europeans arrived eager to understand nature, of course, and also to catalog and explain it; they brought artists with them to create illustrations of nature in the field or trained Americans to produce visual imagery that could help inform Europeans about what the Western Hemisphere looked like. An emerging generation of early modern Atlanticists has been looking at such sources to explain European attitudes toward American nature (among other things) and, to a somewhat lesser extent, American views of colonization, conquest, and the natural world of the Western Hemisphere. Even works that do not seem, on the surface, to be likely sources for environmental historians contain a great deal of information. The conquistador Hernán Cortés's correspondence, published in an excellent modern translation by Anthony Pagden as *Letters from Mexico* (New Haven, Conn., 1991), includes the Spaniard's detailed description of the Aztec emperor Moctezuma's aviary and bestiary, as well as human efforts to contain nature that paralleled—and arguably exceeded—the efforts of Europeans, including

Pope Leo X, who was famous for the Vatican zoo that he created. (Silvio Bedini engagingly tells the story of this collection in *The Pope's Elephant* [New York, 2000].) For revealing new work drawing on such texts, see Emily Berquist Soule, *The Bishop's Utopia: Envisioning Improvement in Colonial Peru* (Philadelphia, 2014), and Neil Safier, *Measuring the New World: Enlightenment Science and South America* (Chicago, 2008).

Some of the travelers to the Americas, including the anonymous authors of the "Histoire Naturelle des Indes" and Sir Walter Ralegh, wrote about the monsters they heard about on the western shores of the Atlantic. These observations need to be understood as one small part of a much larger Atlantic and primarily European conversation about wonders, marvels, and the monstrous. An ideal starting point is with the writings of the sixteenth-century French anatomist Ambroise Paré, whose writings are now available as *On Monsters and Marvels*, trans. Janis L. Pallister (Chicago, 1982). The best studies of European writing about monsters and other wonders and the relationship of these subjects to culture and science include Lorraine Daston and Katherine Park, "Unnatural Conceptions: The Study of Monsters in Sixteenth- and Seventeenth-Century France and England," *Past & Present* 92 (1981), 20–54; idem, *Wonders and the Order of Nature, 1150–1750* (New York, 1998); Stuart Clark, *Thinking with Demons: The Idea of Witchcraft in Early Modern Europe* (Oxford, 1997); and Stephen Greenblatt, *Marvelous Possessions: The Wonder of the New World* (Chicago, 1992). David D. Hall examines similar themes for seventeenth-century North America in *Worlds of Wonders, Days of Judgment: Popular Religious Beliefs in Early New England* (New York, 1989). Michael Camille, in *Image on the Edge: The Margins of Medieval Art* (Cambridge, Mass., 1992), explores the visual marginalia of medieval Europe with dazzling erudition. There has been a recent boom in studies of monsters on maps and other surviving visual evidence. For this work, see, among others, Joseph

Nigg, *Sea Monsters: A Voyage Around the World's Most Beguiling Map* (Chicago, 2013); Boria Sax, *Imaginary Animals: The Monstrous, the Wondrous and the Human* (London, 2013); Chet Van Duzer, *Sea Monsters on Medieval and Renaissance Maps* (London, 2013); and especially Surekha Davies, *Renaissance Ethnography and the Invention of the Human* (Cambridge, Eng., 2016). The art historian Naomi Reed Kline reveals the range of monstrous images that could appear on a single large image; see her *Maps of Medieval Thought: The Hereford Paradigm* (Woodbridge, Suffolk, 2001).

A variety of new works suggest the wide range of relationships between humans and the nonhuman world, an area of much evocative work in recent years. For excellent examples, see Rebecca Kugel, "Of Missionaries and Their Cattle: Ojibwa Perceptions of a Missionary as Evil Shaman," *Ethnohistory* 41 (1994), 227–244; Marcy Norton, "The Chicken or the *Iegue*: Human-Animal Relationships and the Columbian Exchange," *American Historical Review* 120 (2015), 28–60; and the gloriously illustrated study by the anthropologist Shepard Krech III, *Spirits of the Air: Birds and American Indians in the South* (Athens, Ga., 2009). Such studies necessarily transcend the chronological boundaries of the sixteenth century. They remind us, to use the words of the avian enthusiast Jeremy Mynott (who paraphrased the anthropologist Claude Lévi-Strauss), that "birds are good to think with." See Mynott, *Birds in Our Imagination and Experience* (Princeton, N.J., 2009). For a remarkable survey of assessments of birds in early North America, see Elsa G. Allen, "The History of American Ornithology Before Audubon," *Transactions of the American Philosophical Society* 41 (1951), 387–591.

Many of these books make clear the central importance of visual evidence to any understanding of nature in the early modern Atlantic basin. Pictures are crucial for more than understanding nature. As Anthony Grafton and his colleagues revealed at the time of the Columbian quincentennial in *New Worlds, Ancient Texts: The Power of Tradition and the Shock of Discovery* (Cambridge, Mass., 1992), engravings in particular played a major role in Europeans' understanding of both the news coming from the Americas and how such novel information could be integrated into existing frames of reference that had developed in Antiquity. Yet scholars of the sixteenth-century Atlantic basin, with the exception of art historians for whom depictions of American nature have been a primary focus, have not spent much time on surviving images. Perhaps the work of those who have can provide a model. See, among the richly illustrated analyses by art historians, Serge Gruzinski, *Painting the Conquest: The Mexican Indians and the European Renaissance* (Paris, 1992); Donna Pierce, Rogelio Ruiz Gomar, and Clara Bargellini, *Painting a New World: Mexican Art and Life, 1521–1821* (Denver, Colo., 2004); and Michael Gaudio's exceptional *Engraving the Savage: The New World and Techniques of Civilization* (Minneapolis, Minn., 2008).

Visual evidence, like textual information, cannot be read only on the surface. Instead, each image needs to be understood as part of a genre. Artists frequently borrowed motifs from one another, and specific imagery took on iconic status when it moved back and forth between painters, sculptors, and engravers. As art historians have demonstrated, images moved from one artist to another, crossing the boundaries between media effectively. Hence Diana Magaloni Kerpel has suggested how a copy of Pliny's natural history shaped the artistic strategies of Nahua artists in the 1570s; see *The Colors of the New World: Artists, Materials, and the Creation of the* Florentine Codex (Los Angeles, 2014). More commonly, images of the monstrous, as the inspired art historian Rudolf Wittkower argued two generations ago in his astonishing essay "Marvels of the East: A Study in the History of Monsters," *Journal of the Warburg and Courtauld Institutes* 5 (1942), 159–197, migrated from one venue to another. Such visual translations occurred ever more frequently with the expansion of print, which coincided with Europeans' enduring, and one might even suggest expanding, interest in unusual or difficult to explain phenomena.

Art historians' insights, then, prepare the viewer for understanding visual evidence from the sixteenth-century Atlantic basin. The creators of the "Vallard Atlas" did not need to go to Africa to see what an elephant looked like when they placed a gray elephant, its long tusks leading the way, in the interior of their map of southern Africa (folio 5) because they already knew how the creature looked. By the time the unknown creators of the "Histoire Naturelle des Indes" painted their watercolors, which included reptiles of various sizes, they might have seen Old World crocodiles. There was even a desiccated specimen hanging in the cathedral in Seville. It is still there today, although at some point the original was replaced by a wooden model.

Fortunately, much of the visual evidence I have drawn on here can be found in modern editions. Arthur J. O. Anderson and Charles E. Dibble have translated and edited Bernardino Sahagún's work as *General History of the Things of New Spain: Florentine Codex*, published by the School of American Research in thirteen parts (Santa Fe and Salt Lake City, 1950–1982). The Huntington's manuscript of the "Vallard Atlas" can be found in a spectacular facsimile, with an accompanying companion volume, edited by Manuel Moliero (Barcelona, 2010). Moliero has also produced a similar high-quality reproduction of the 1519 "Atlas Miller" (in three parts [Barcelona, 2006]), which contains crucial early sixteenth-century visual representations of the Western Hemisphere with significant images of both Brazil and Canada. The "Histoire Naturelle des Indes," which resides at the Morgan Library in New York, has been reproduced as *The Drake Manuscript*, with a translation of the original text by Ruth S. Kraemer (London, 1996). The watercolors painted by John White in Roanoke in 1585 are beautifully reproduced in David Beers

Quinn and Paul Hulton, eds., *The American Drawings of John White, 1577–1590: With Drawings of European and Oriental Subjects*, 2 vols. (Chapel Hill, N.C., 1964). Many scholars have written about these images and the context of their production and use, an interest driven in part by the 400th anniversary in 2007 of the establishment of Jamestown. See especially Kim Sloan, *A New World: England's First View of America* (Chapel Hill, N.C., 2007). The best study of the workings of the de Bry workshop is Michiel van Groesen's *The Representations of the Overseas World in the de Bry Collection of Voyages (1590–1634)* (Leiden, 2008). Susan Scott Parrish's *American Curiosity: Cultures of Natural History in the Colonial British Atlantic World* (Chapel Hill, N.C., 2006) follows the story of some of the crucial images beyond 1600.

Yet despite the availability of many sixteenth-century sources, much remains little known. The cloister at Fréjus has yet to be subjected to intensive academic study; the only published books on the subject—other than studies about the Roman foundations and baptismal font of the Cathédrale St. Léonce—are two relatively brief guidebooks: Colette Dumas and Georges Puchal, *L'imagier de Fréjus: Les plafonds du cloître de la cathédrale* (Paris, 2001) and Michel Fixot, *Fréjus: La cathédrale Saint-Léonce et le groupe épiscopal* (Paris, 2004). More common are studies of the origins and early development of the cathedral, such as Lucien Rivet, Daniel Bretchaloff, and Jacques Gascou, "Compléments aux "ILN-Fréjus—2. Fouilles de la cathédrale (1987–1988)," *Zeitshcrif für Papyrologie und Epigraphik* 155 (2006), 263–267, and Michel Fichot, ed., *Le groupe épiscopale de Fréjus* (Turnhout, Belgium, 2012). The "Histoire Naturelle des Indes," despite the existence of the facsimile, has been used by some specialists but, like the "Vallard," this treasure from the Morgan Library remains at the margins of scholars' frame of reference. A notable and delightful exception to this lack of attention is Janice Neri's exquisite *The Insect and the Image: Visualizing Nature in Early Mod-*

ern Europe, 1500–1700 (Minneapolis, Minn., 2011), which analyzes both Topsell and the "Histoire Naturelle" from the perspective of a scholar on the ever-expansive borderland of the history of art and the history of science. For more on the intersection of those once distinct scholarly fields, see Lorraine J. Daston, ed., *Things That Talk: Object Lessons from Art and Science* (New York, 2007); David Freedberg, *The Eye of the Lynx: Galileo, His Friends, and the Beginnings of Modern Natural History* (Chicago, 2002); and Sachiko Kusukawa, *Picturing the Book of Nature: Image, Text, and Argument in Sixteenth-Century Human Anatomy and Medical Botany* (Chicago, 2012). But Topsell still remains relatively understudied. There is no complete edition of his elegant *Fowles of Heaven*, his updated English-language version of Aldrovandi's *Ornithologiae*, for which the manuscript for the only completed part (from A through C; he got hung up on chickens and cocks) is at the Huntington (EL 1142). For a facsimile of part of the work, see Topsell, *The Fowles of Heaven; or History of Birdes*, ed. Thomas P. Harrison and F. David Hoeniger (Austin, Tex., 1972). Still, neither Topsell's nor Thomas Moffet's major work has appeared in a scholarly edition since 1658, which is perhaps not all that surprising except for the fact that some comparable herbals have been produced in modern editions—such as Leonart Fuchs, *The New Herbal of 1543* (Köln, 2001), and William Turner, *A New Herbal*, ed. George T. L. Chapman and Marilyn N. Tweddle, 2 vols. (Cambridge, Eng., 1996). Moffet has attracted some, although not enough, scholarly attention; see V. H. Houliston, "Sleepers Awake: Thomas Moffet's Challenge to the College of Physicians of London, 1584," *Medical History* 33 (1989), 235–246. For Topsell, see Bayard H. Christy, "Topsell's 'Fowles of Heaven,'" *Auk* 50 (1933), 275–283, and Katherine Acheston, "Gesner, Topsell, and the Purposes of Pictures in Early Modern Natural Histories," in Michael Hunter, ed., *Printed Images in Early Modern Britain: Essays in Interpretation* (London, 2010), 127–144, which situates Topsell between Gesner, whose *Historiae Animalium* (4 vols., 1551–1558) was the greatest work of natural history in early modern Europe to that point, and the naturalists and illustrators who drew on Topsell's book, with differing degrees of fidelity to the text and its illustrations.

More poignantly, the environmental history of sixteenth-century Africa remains a topic that has barely penetrated the works of scholars of the era. The "Vallard Atlas" has three maps (folios 5–7) that depict Africa—one of parts of northwest Africa, which includes a depiction of the modern Middle East; one for the southern reaches of the continent; and a third showing West Africa. These maps contain European ideas about what could be found on the continent, including well-built cities (the palace of the legendary Prester John), elephants, lions, tigers, monkeys, crocodiles, thick stands of trees, and (in the last of these maps), two monsters talking to each other and one ape who seems to be juggling in front of an unidentified potentate. These images were accurate only in the sense that artists depicted on these pages what they had already learned about Africa, presumably from Europeans who traveled there or Africans who had journeyed northward. Such travel, while perhaps not quite common, was a well-known phenomenon by the sixteenth century, as David Northrup reveals in *Africa's Discovery of Europe, 1450–1850* (New York, 2002).

Yet to date, the environmental history of early modern, especially pre-1600, Africa lags behind what scholars have produced for other parts of the world. John F. Richards's *The Unending Frontier: An Environmental History of the Early Modern World* (Berkeley, Calif., 2003), an otherwise colossal guide, contains but a single chapter on Africa, and it focuses on southern Africa and primarily in the period after the arrival of the Dutch. Judith A. Carney, *Black Rice: The African Origins of Rice Cultivation in the Americas* (Cambridge, Mass., 2001), traces the earliest appearance of Old World rice in the Americas and the ways that information about how to cultivate the plant likely traveled swiftly in the sixteenth century, although most of the book treats the period after 1600. James C. McCann, *Maize and Grace: Africa's Encounter with a New World Crop, 1500–2000* (Cambridge, Mass., 2005), pursues an opposite phenomenon—an American crop taking hold in Africa—but most of it addresses the post-1600 period. William Beinert's superb review of African environmental history confirms that most twentieth-century works focused on the period after 1600; see his "African History and Environmental History," *African Affairs* 99 (2000), 269–302. The source material for studies of the sixteenth century is rich, especially for scholars willing to combine indigenous knowledge and contemporary accounts, such as travel narratives, which often described both natural resources and how locals used them. Although these works do not concentrate on this era, see Tamara Giles-Vernick, *Cutting Vines of the Past: Environmental Histories of the Central African Rain Forest* (Charlottesville, Va., 2002); Judith Carney and Nicholas Rosomoff, *In the Shadow of Slavery: Africa's Botanical Legacy in the Atlantic World* (Berkeley, Calif., 2011); Walter Hawthorne, *Planting Rice and Harvesting Slaves: Transformations Along the Guinea-Bissau Coast, 1400–1900* (London, 2003); and, for northern Africa, Alan Mikhail, *Nature and Empire in Ottoman Egypt: An Environmental History* (New York, 2011).

Similarly, there is far less material about sixteenth-century indigenous American views of nature than for Europeans' interpretations, although the surviving codices from sixteenth-century Mexico provide crucial details. In addition to the material in the *Florentine Codex* on insects, a series of texts provides clues into the ways that Americans understood nature. The list of tributes in the "Codex Mendoza," for example, testifies to the value of specific high-value commodities such as jade and jaguar pelts. As the "Mendoza" made its way into Europe—first in the hands of the French royal cosmographer André Thevet in Paris and then to the English editor Richard Hakluyt, whose papers after his death came into the possession of a minister named Samuel Purchas, who then published an engraved version of the illustrations from the "Mendoza" (but lacking its earlier Spanish commentary)—knowledge about the riches to be found in Mexico found a wider audience. To understand how and where these codices migrated, see Daniela Bleichmar, "History in Pictures: Translating the *Codex Mendoza,*" *Art History* 38 (2015), 682–701, and Peter Mason, *The Lives of Images* (London, 2001). For traces of indigenous Brazilian conceptualizations of aspects of nature, see Eduardo Kohn, *How Forests Think: Toward an Anthropology Beyond the Human* (Berkeley, Calif., 2013).

But the series of events that preserved the information in the "Mendoza," from the original transcribing of indigenous knowledge and tribute systems through the translation of the manuscript across the Atlantic Ocean and eventually into the hands of an engraver, was not replicated frequently. There is, as a result, a relative dearth of indigenous visual material for much of the Western Hemisphere. Scholars keen to get beyond the lacuna need to find ways to use oral history, archaeological remains, or folklore to interpret earlier understandings of the natural world. To do so requires breaking through the hold of Western historical traditions, which emphasize the primacy of contemporary written documents. From this perspective, the stories that the English explorer Sir Walter Ralegh heard about the monsters roaming the Orinoco basin need to be set alongside the stories of the monstrous to be found in the fourteenth-century paintings at Fréjus and the medical observations of Ambroise Paré. Similarly, local legends about how long a Caribbean pearl diver could swim under water—another idea captured in the "Histoire Naturelle des Indes"—need to be understood in a European context about the search for valuable *naturalia*.

There is an abundant catalog of indigenous American oral history, much of it concerned with explaining how certain parts of a landscape came into existence. These verbal descriptions are crucial to understand peoples whose religious concepts often pivoted on identifying some places or entities as possessing spiritual power, a notion that still holds among many indigenous people and has become central in legal arguments about the preservation and use of specific resources. (For more on the legal history within the United States, see N. Bruce Duthu, *American Indians and the Law* [New York, 2007].) A walrus might be desirable to a European hunter, but the spirits that controlled the movements of walrus in the sea or a reindeer on land needed to be propitiated lest mistreating a corpse led to a failure to capture the next walrus or reindeer. Nonnative observers like the American ship captain Charles Francis Hall often dismissed such beliefs as savage superstition, as can be seen in his works, notably *Life with the Esquimaux: The Narrative of Captain Charles Francis Hall, of the* Whaling Barque "George Henry" (London, 1864) and *Narrative of the Second Arctic Expedition* (Washington, D.C., 1879). Stripped of their authors' own biases, such narratives testify to long-held indigenous beliefs about how to live in particular places. An excellent introduction to this literature is Peter Nabokov, ed., *Native American Testimony*, rev. ed. (New York, 1999). For works that draw on precontact cultures with particular success, see Alvin M. Josephy Jr., ed., *America in 1492: The World of the Indian Peoples Before the Arrival of Columbus* (New York, 1991); Lisa Brooks, *The Common Pot: The Recovery of Native Space in the Northeast* (Minneapolis, Minn., 2008); and William S. Simmons, *Spirit of the New England Tribes: Indian History and Folklore, 1620–1984* (Lebanon, N.H., 1986). In a related vein, see Shepard Krech III, *The Ecological Indian: Myth and History* (New York, 1999), a study that looks at both legend and environmental history.

Early modern scholars and environmental historians have recognized the seventeenth and eighteenth centuries as marking a pivotal moment in the ways that humans reconceptualized their views of nature. In addition to Worster's foundational work in *Nature's Economy*, those interested in this era would benefit from three superb works: Fredrik A. Jonsson, *Enlightenment's Frontier: The Scottish Origins of Environmentalism* (New Haven, Conn., 2013); Carolyn Merchant, *Ecological Revolutions: Nature, Gender, and Science in New England* (Chapel Hill, N.C., 1989); and Richard Grove, *Green Imperialism: Colonial Expansion, Tropical Island Edens and the Origins of Environmentalism, 1600–1800* (Cambridge, Eng., 1995).

Now it is time to push inquiries into the sixteenth century and to integrate visual images and oral history into the canon of acceptable evidence for understanding the complex relationship between culture and nature during the century when the peoples of the Atlantic basin met each other on a sustained basis. The planet has not been the same since.

NOTES

PREFACE

1. Edward Topsell, *The Historie of Serpents* (London, 1608), 90.

2. For the complexities of the shift and the simultaneous existence of multiple views of nature and what constituted phenomena beyond, see the paradigm-defining work by Lorraine Daston and Katherine Park, *Wonders and the Order of Nature, 1150–1750* (New York, 1998). Their study focuses almost exclusively on Europe; there is no comparable work for the Americas or for the Atlantic basin.

3. Stephen Greenblatt, *The Swerve: How the World Became Modern* (New York, 2011). Greenblatt's study pivots on the rediscovery of Lucretius's *On the Nature of Things*; for more on that subject, see Ada Palmer's perceptive *Reading Lucretius in the Renaissance* (Cambridge, Mass., 2014). For the most thoughtful effort to trace similarities between precontact North America and Europe, see Daniel K. Richter, *Before the Revolution: America's Ancient Pasts* (Cambridge, Mass., 2011), esp. 11–64.

4. Alfred W. Crosby, *The Columbian Exchange: Biological and Cultural Consequences of 1492* (Westport, Conn., 1972).

5. Donald Worster, *Shrinking the Earth: The Rise and Decline of American Abundance* (New York, 2016), 5–6.

6. Diana Magaloni Kerpel, *The Colors of the New World: Artists, Materials, and the Creation of the* Florentine Codex (Los Angeles, 2014), 19–20, 51–52.

CHAPTER ONE

1. Walter Ralegh, "The discoverie of the large, rich, and beautifull Empire of Guiana," in Richard Hakluyt, *The Principal Navigations Voyages Traffiques and Discoveries of the English Nation*, 3 vols. (London, 1598–1600), III: 652–653 (ewaipanoma), 638 (Amazons).

2. Surekha Davies, *Renaissance Ethnography and the Invention of the Human: New Worlds, Maps, and Monsters* (Cambridge, Eng., 2016); Chet Van

Duzer, *Sea Monsters on Medieval and Renaissance Maps* (London, 2013); Joseph Nigg, *Sea Monsters: A Voyage Around the World's Most Beguiling Map* (Chicago, 2013).

3. Ambroise Paré, *On Monsters and Marvels*, trans. Janis L. Pallister (Chicago, 1982).

4. The most thorough discussion, which draws on an extraordinary number of examples across Europe, is Daston and Park, *Wonders and the Order of Nature, 1150–1750*, 173–214.

5. The growing interest in the East in particular replaced an earlier emphasis on the North, especially in Ireland; see Daston and Park, *Wonders and the Order of Nature,* 25–27. On Europeans' engagement with the Global South and their ideas that climate contributed to the creation of monsters, see Nicolás Wey-Gómez, *The Tropics of Discourse: Why Columbus Sailed South to the Indies* (Cambridge, Mass., 2008), 84–86 and 218–221.

6. See, e.g., Isaiah 27:1; Lamentations 4:3; Job 3:8, 7:12, 26:12; Psalm 74:13; and, most famously, Revelation chapters 12 and 13.

7. Rudolf Wittkower, "Marvels of the East: A Study in the History of Monsters," *Journal of the Warburg and Courtauld Institutes* 5 (1942), 159–197.

8. See Carolyn Walker Bynum, "Wonder," *American Historical Review* 102 (1997), 1–17.

9. See Michael Camille, *Image on the Edge: The Margins of Medieval Art* (Cambridge, Mass., 1992), esp. 77–97.

10. Lucretius, *On the Nature of Things*, trans. W. H. D. Rouse, revised by Martin F. Smith (Cambridge, Mass., 1992), 335 (centaur), 269 (Cerberus, furies, Tartarus), 449 (Scylla and chimera).

11. See, e.g., Robert Bartlett, *The Natural and the Supernatural in the Middle Ages* (Cambridge, Eng., 2008), 94–110. On the rediscovery of Lucretius, see Greenblatt, *The Swerve.*

12. See, e.g., Michel Pastoureau, *Bestiaires du Moyen Âge* (Paris, 2011), *passim*; René Cintré, *Bestiaire médiévale des animaux familiers* (Rennes, 2013), 18.

13. Konrad [of Megenberg], [*Buch der Natur*], [Augsburg, 1475] (Huntington Library [hereafter HEH] 85861).

14. See Eva Matthews Sanford, "The Liber Floridus," *Catholic Historical Review* 26 (1941), 469–478; Jessie Poesch, "The Beasts from Job in the *Liber Floridus* Manuscripts," *Journal of the Warburg and Courtauld Institutes* 33 (1970), 41–51.

15. *The Travels of John Mandeville*, trans. C. W. R. D. Mosely (London, 1983), 9–12; for the deep context, which situates Pliny's views among other ancient travelers' views of what they saw as exotic lands, see James S. Romm, *The Edges of the Earth in Ancient Thought* (Princeton, N.J., 1992), esp. 83–120.

16. See [Jean Frederic Bernard], *Cérémonies, moeurs, et coutumes religieuses de tous les peuples du monde*, 7 vols. (Paris, 1741), 7: 103.

17. See Jules Charles-Roux, *Notes historiques sur Fréjus* (orig. pub. 1909; rpt. Paris, 2001). Even a modern guidebook to the church has only a relatively short section on the cloister; see Michel Fixot, *La cathédrale Saint-Léonce et le groupe episcopal de Fréjus* (Paris, 2004), 50–57.

18. Jacques Maretz, "Carte de la côte de Provence" (1633) in Olivier Chapuis, *Cartes des côtes de France: Histoire de la cartographie marine et terrestre du littoral* (Douarnenez, Brittany, 2007), 62–63.

19. Colette Dumas and Georges Puchal, *L'imagier de Fréjus: Les plafonds du cloître de la cathédrale* (Paris, 2001), 27.

20. Jean-Nöel Biraben, *Les Hommes et la peste en France et dans les pays européens et méediterranéens, Tome I: La peste dans l'histoire* (Paris, 1975), 377–378. For the arrival and initial spread of the plague in France, see Henry Dubois, "La depression: XIVe et XVe siècles," in Jacques Dupâquier, ed., *Histoire de la population Française*, vol. 1, *Des origens à la Renaissance* (Paris, 1988), esp. the map on 315.

21. Dumas and Puchal, *L'imagier de Fréjus*, 42–47.

22. Dumas and Puchas, *L'imagier de Fréjus*, 48–53.

23. Dumas and Puchas, *L'imagier de Fréjus*, 56–67. On the popularity of dog-headed humans, see Bartlett, *The Natural and the Supernatural*, 94–102.

24. The process is visible in many places, but for fine examples, see the layers in the foundation of the Notre-Dame-de-Nazareth Cathedral in Vaison La Romaine or the church, now mostly abandoned, at Valles des Nymphes. For the former, see Christian Goudineau and Yves de Kisch, *Archaeological Guide to Vaison La Romaine* (Vaison-la-Romaine, 1984), 80–83.

25. See Peter Low, "'You Who Once Were Far Off': Enlivening Sculpture in the Main Portal at Vézelay," *Art Bulletin* 85 (2003), 469–489, esp. 470.

26. The most informed summary can be found in Wittkower, "Marvels of the East."

27. See Naomi Reed Kline, *Maps of Medieval Thought: The Hereford Paradigm* (Woodbridge, Suffolk, 2001), 141–164.

28. For one excellent image of a blemmye, a sciopod, and a "wild man," see the image of the monstrous races from c. 1400 in *Bibliothèque nationale de France*, MS fr. 2810, f. 29v; the image is reprinted as picture 4 in the gallery between pages 130 and 131 in John Larner, *Marco Polo and the Discovery of the World* (New Haven, Conn., 1999), and in Bynum, "Wonder," 21.

29. *Travels of John Mandeville*, trans. Moseley, 9.

30. Ralegh, "Discoverie of Guiana," in Hakluyt, *Principal Navigations*, III: 653.

31. *Travels of Mandeville*, trans. Moseley, 9–12.

32. *Othello*, Act I, scene 3, lines 142–143.

33. Columbus, "The Barcelona Letter of 1493," trans. Lucia Graves, in Mauricio Obregón, ed., *The Columbus Papers: The Barcelona Letter of 1493, the Landfall Controversy, and the Indian Guides* (New York, 1991), 67.

34. Valerie Flint, *Imaginative Landscape of Christopher Columbus* (Princeton, N.J., 1992), 151–154, quotation at 154.

35. Giuliano Dati, *El Secondo Cantare* ([Rome, 1494 or 1495]), sigs. [1v], [2v], [2r]. According to *European Americana*, there are only two known copies of this version, one in the Biblioteca Casanatense in Rome and the other in the Lilly Library at Indiana University; I used one of the ten photostats of the Roman copy produced in 1922, which dates the text to 1494 (HEH 47258). (The text is also available online at the Biblioteca Europea di Informatione e Cultura.) The last woodcut in this brief work depicts a king on an elephant, another detail absent from Columbus's report; see sig. [4r]. For a translation of the first edition, *Lettera delle isole nuovamente trovate* (Florence, 1493), see Martin Davies, trans., *Columbus in Italy: An Italian Versification of the Letter on the Discovery of the New World* (London, 1991), 33–40.

36. The *Nuremburg Chronicle* included two plates depicting the monstrous races to be found at the far margins of Europeans' world; see Hartmann Schedel, *The Book of Chronicles: The Complete and Annotated* Nuremburg Chronicle *of 1493*, ed. Stephan Füssel (Köln, 2013), plates xii–xiii. See also Anthony Grafton, *New Worlds, Ancient Texts: The Power of Tradition and the Shock of Discovery* (Cambridge, Mass., 1992), 35–42.

37. "The Medieval West and the Indian Ocean: An Oneiric Horizon," in Jacques Le Goff, *Time, Work, and Culture in the Middle Ages* (Chicago, 1980), 190.

38. See Daston and Park, *Wonders and the Order of Nature*, 173–214.

39. Stuart Clark, *Thinking with Demons: The Idea of Witchcraft in Early Modern Europe* (Oxford, 1997), 363–374.

40. The story of Paré and his intellectual and working milieu can be found in Janis L. Pallister's superb introduction to her translation of the work, published as *Ambroise Paré on Monsters and Marvels* (Chicago, 1982), xvi–xxv.

41. Pallister, trans., *Paré on Monsters and Marvels*, 3–4 (causes of monsters), 38–42 (monsters caused by imagination), 49–60 (items produced within human bodies); Michelle Karnes, "Marvels in the Medieval Imagination," *Speculum* 90 (2015), 327–366.

42. Pallister, trans., *Paré on Monsters and Marvels*, 67–73.

43. Bert Hansen, *Nicole Oresme and the Marvels of Nature: A Study of his* De causis mirabilium *with Critical Edition, Translation, and Commentary*, Pontifical Institute of Mediaeval Studies—Studies and Texts 68 (Toronto, 1985), 229–249, quotation at 237.

44. See Flint, *Imaginative Landscape*, 53–54.

45. *The excellent and pleasant worke of Julius Solinus Polyhistor*, trans. Arthur Golding (London, 1587), sig. Dv4r.

46. Rondolet, *L'histoire entiere des poissons* (Lyon, 1558), 358–362.

47. André Thevet, *La cosmographie universelle*, 2 vols. (Paris, 1575), II: 941, 980v, 992, 1002.

48. The map has been reproduced in a modern facsimile: see *Olai Magni Gothi Carta marina et descriptio septemtrionalium terrarum ac mirabilium rerum in eis contentarum* (Malmö, [1949]) (HEH 762294).

49. See Olaus Magnus, *Historia de gentibus septentrionalibus* (Romae, 1555), trans. as *Description of the Northern Peoples*, ed. Peter Foote, 3 vols. Hakluyt Society, 2nd ser., vols. 182, 187, and 188 (London, 1996–1998), I: 101–102, 164–166, and book 21, which focused on what he called "sea monsters," a term that alternated between monstrous (i.e., seemingly unnatural) and large creatures (such as whales), III: 1081–1139, *passim*.

50. Edward Topsell, *The Historie of Four-Footed Beastes* (London, 1607), 281–435 (horses), 661–705 (swine), 44–50 (beaver), 17–19 (sphinx), 12–15 (satyr), 711–721 (unicorn), 660 (su); Topsell, *Historie of Serpents*, 158–173 (winged dragon).

51. Topsell, "The Fowles of Heaven," EL 1142, HEH, quotation at f. 3v.

52. Topsell, "Fowles of Heaven," f. 22r–v. He cited Ramusio, whom he labeled "a grate Travayler of Venice." See also Elsa G. Allen, "The History of American Ornithology Before Audubon," *Transactions of the American Philosophical Society* 41 (1951), 448–449.

53. Topsell, "Fowles of Heaven," 60v. For the context, see Ulisse Aldrovandi, *Aldrovandi on Chickens*, trans. and ed. L. R. Lind (Norman, Okla., 1963), and Caroline Duroselle-Melish and David A. Lines, "The Library of Ulisse Aldrovandi († 1605): Acquiring and Organizing Books in Sixteenth-Century Bologna," *The Library*, 7th ser., 16: 2 (June, 2015), 133–161.

54. Topsell, "Fowles of Heaven," f. 85r (Chuguareo), f. 85v (Chuwheeo), f. 86r (Chowankus and Chungent); Bayard H. Christy, "Topsell's Fowles of Heaven," *Auk* 50 (1933), 275–283, provided modern names for the birds in Topsell's manuscript and identified the towhee as the picture of the bird the naturalist received from Hakluyt.

55. Topsell, "Fowles of Heaven," f. 32r.

56. Topsell, "Fowles of Heaven," f.35r (bat),

57. Topsell, "Fowles of Heaven," ff. 115r–201r, especially ff. 127v–128v (monstrous cocks), f. 127r (five-footed cock), f. 126v (hen with four legs), f. 126r (four-footed cock), f. 125r (three-footed hen), f. 124r–v (three-footed cocks).

58. On Hakluyt and Ramusio, see Peter C. Mancall, *Hakluyt's Promise: An Elizabethan's Obsession for an English America* (New Haven, Conn., 2007), 86–88, 93, 141–142.

59. Paré, *Monsters and Marvels*, trans. Pallister, 116–118, 119, 121, 139, 141, 144, 146, 166–167; Mancall, *Hakluyt's Promise* (Thevet and Hakluyt), 47–48; Thevet, *La cosmographie universelle*, 2 vols. (Paris, 1575), II: 965v–968r.

60. Hakluyt, *The Principall Navigations, Voiages, and Travels of the English Nation* (London, 1589), 25–79 (Mandeville); Hakluyt, *Principal Navigations*, III: 627–662 (Ralegh on the Orinoco); Ralegh, *Brevis & Admiranda description Regni Guianæ Avri Abundantissimi, in America* (Nuremburg, 1599) (the Hulsius edition of Ralegh's account); Rondolet, *L'histoire entiere des poissons*, sig. a 4r.

61. Daston and Park, *Wonders and the Order of Nature*, 173–214.

62. See, e.g., Charles Stevens and John Leibault, *Maison Rustique: Or, The Countrey Farme*, trans. Richard Surflet (London, 1606).

63. Magnus, *A Description of the Northern Peoples* (1555), ed. Foote, 3: 173.

64. For the ritual and its place in Venetian life, see Edward Muir, *Civic Ritual in Renaissance Venice* (Princeton, N.J., 1981), 119–134.

65. See, e.g., Paulo Zacchia, *Questiones Medico-Legales* (Frankfurt, 1666), 526–534.

66. My ideas on the flow of information from one generation to the next have been shaped primarily by Bernard Bailyn, *Education in the Forming of American Society* (Chapel Hill, N.C., 1960).

67. As Ramusio put it in the opening of his collection of travel accounts that included the Western Hemisphere: "Se ne trovano case publiche piene di dette corde, con le quai facilme[n]te da ad inte[n]der colui, che n'ha il carico, le cose passate, ben che elle siano di molta eta avanti di lui: si come noi facciamo con le nostre lettere"; see Ramusio, *Terzo volume della navigationi et viaggi* ([Venice, 1556]), 4r.

68. Jean de Léry, *Historia Indiae Occidentalis, tomis duobis comprehensa* ([Geneva], 1586).

69. For an analysis, see Benjamin Schmidt, "Reading Ralegh's America: Texts, Books, and Readers in the Early Modern Atlantic World," in Peter C. Mancall, ed., *The Atlantic World and Virginia, 1550–1624* (Chapel Hill, N.C., 2007), 473–481; for the ways that American creatures continued to fascinate English observers, see Susan Scott Parrish, *American Curiosity: Cultures of Natural History in the Colonial British Atlantic World* (Chapel Hill, N.C., 2006).

70. George Kubler, "Serpent and Atlantean Columns: Symbols of Maya-Toltec Polity," *Journal of the Society of Architectural Historians* XLI (1982), 93–115, quotation at 93; see also Paul Gendrop, *Rio Bec, Chenes, and Puuc Styles in Maya Architecture*, trans. Robert D. Wood, ed. George F. Andrews (Lancaster, Calif., 1998), 69–74, and Jeffrey Chouinard, *Mouths of Stone: Stories of the Ancient Maya from Newly Deciphered Inscriptions and Recent Archaeological Discoveries* (Durham, N.C., 1995).

71. Cynthia Kristan-Graham and Jeff Karl Kowalski, "Chichén Itzá, Tula, and Tollan: Changing Perspectives on a Recurring Problem in Mesoamerican Archaeology and Art History," in Kowalski and Kristan-Graham, eds., *Twin Tollans: Chichén Itzá, Tula, and the Epiclassic to Early Postclassic Mesoamerican World* (Washington, D.C., 2011), 1. (I thank Joanne Pillsbury for this reference.)

72. See, e.g., Oswaldo Chinchilla Mazariegos, "Of Birds and Insects: The Hummingbird Myth in Ancient Mesoamerica," *Ancient Mesoamerica* 21 (2010), 45–61.

73. Catherine L. Albanese, *Nature Religion in America: From the Algonkian Indians to the New Age* (Chicago, 1990), 19–25, quotation at 21; N. Scott Momaday, *The Way to Rainy Mountain* (orig. pub. 1969; rpt. Albuquerque, N.M., 1976), 6–8, quotation at 8; Kerpel, *The Colors of the New World*, 12–13.

74. Elizabeth Fenn, *Encounters at the Heart of the World: A History of the Mandan People* (New York, 2014), 119.

75. C. M. Barbeau, *Huron and Wyandot Mythology*, number 11 in the Anthropological Series of the Canada Department of Mines Geological Survey (Ottawa, 1915), 56–58.

76. Lynn Ceci, "Watchers of the Pleiades: Ethnoastronomy Among Native Cultivators in Northeastern North America," *Ethnohistory* 25 (1978), 301–317.

77. Albanese, *Nature Religion*, 23; Deacon Phineas Field, "Stories, Anecdotes and Legends," in *History and Proceedings of the Pocumtuck Valley Memorial Association, 1870–1879* (Deerfield, Mass., 1890), I: 62–63; George Sheldon, *A History of Deerfield, Massachusetts*, 2 vols. (Deerfield, Mass., 1895), I: 29; and Margaret M. Bruchac, "Earthshapers and Placemakers: Algonkian Indian Stories and the Landscape," in Claire Smith and H. Martin Wobst, eds., *Indigenous Archaeologies: Decolonizing Theory and Practice* (London, 2005), 69–73 (Pocumtuck), 62–63 (Penobscot Bay); Thoreau, *The Maine Woods* (orig. pub. 1864; rpt. New York, 1985), 724–725.

78. Fenn, *Encounters at the Heart of the World*, 4–6.

79. Shepard Krech III, *Spirits of the Air: Birds & American Indians in the South* (Athens, Ga., 2009), 167–169, quotation at 167.

80. Paul told the stories to the anthropologist W. H. Mechling, who gathered oral legends from 1910 to 1912 and published them as *Malecite Tales*, number 4 in the Anthropological Series of the Geological Survey of the Canada Department of Mines (Ottawa, 1914); these incidents are related on 1–2.

81. Sagard, *The Long Journey to the Country of the Hurons*, trans. H. H. Langton, ed. George M. Wrong, Publications of the Champlain Society 25 (Toronto, 1939), 171.

82. Paul Le Jeune, *Relation de ce qui s'est passé en La Nouvelle France en*

L'Anee 1633 (Paris, 1634), trans. in Reuben Gold Thwaites, *The Jesuit Relations and Allied Documents*, 93 vols. (Cleveland, Ohio, 1896–1901), V: 152–157.

83. See, e.g., the various kinds of thanksgiving rituals among Iroquois, described in Anthony F. C. Wallace, *The Death and Rebirth of the Seneca* (New York, 1969), 50–59.

84. Daniel K. Richter, *The Ordeal of the Longhouse: The Peoples of the Iroquois League in the Era of European Colonization* (Chapel Hill, N.C., 1992), 24.

85. See Charles Hudson, ed., *The Black Drink: A Native American Tea* (Athens, Ga., 1979).

86. Bruce G. Trigger, *The Children of Aataentsic: A History of the Huron People to 1660*, 2 vols. (Montreal, 1976), I: 77–78.

87. See Cottie A. Borland, "Codex Borbonicus: Pages 21 and 22—A Critical Assessment," *Journal de la Société des Américanistes* 46 (1957), 160.

88. See, e.g., Joseph C. Winter, "From Earth Mother to Snake Woman: The Role of Tobacco in the Evolution of Native American Religious Orientation," in Joseph C. Winter, ed., *Tobacco Use by Native North Americans: Sacred Smoke and Silent Killer* (Norman, Okla., 2000), 265–304.

89. Parsons, "Natives, Newcomers, and *Nicotiana*: Tobacco in the History of the Great Lakes Region," in Robert Englebert and Guillaume Teasdale, eds., *French and Indians in the Heart of North America* (East Lansing, Mich., 2013), 21–41, quotation at 33.

90. Silas Rand, *Legends of the Micmac* (New York, 1894), 228–229.

91. Nicolas Perrot, *Mémoire sur les moeurs, coustumes, et religion des sauvages de L'Amerique septentrionale* (Leipzig and Paris, 1864), 280

92. For these early European reports and how they circulated, see Peter C. Mancall, "Tales Tobacco Told in Sixteenth-Century Europe," *Environmental History* 17 (2004), 648–678.

93. William Cronon, *Changes in the Land: Indians, Colonists, and the Ecology of New England* (New York, 1983), 51.

94. For rabbits (conies), see *The Drake Manuscript in the Pierpont Morgan Library: Histoire Naturelle des Indes* (London, 1996), ff. 95–96; for buffalo, see Shepard Krech III, *The Ecological Indian: Myth and History* (New York, 1999), 127–135.

95. Krech, *Ecological Indian*, 129–130.

96. See, among other sources, Fenn, *Encounters at the Heart of the World*, 65–67.

97. See Calvin Martin, *Keepers of the Game: Indians, Animals, and the Fur Trade* (Berkeley, Calif., 1978), esp. 113–130.

98. Adrian Tanner, *Bringing Home Animals: Religious Ideology and Mode of Production of the Mistassini Cree Hunters* (New York, 1979), 147, 153–181.

99. See Robert McGhee, "Ivory for the Sea Woman: The Symbolic Attributes of a Prehistoric Technology," in Susan M. Pearce, ed., *Interpreting Objects and*

Collections (London, 1994), 59–66; David W. Penny, *Indigenous Beauty: Master-works of American Indian Art from the Diker Collection* (New York, 2015), 64.

100. Fenn, *Encounters at the Heart of the World*, 100.

101. See Thomas Babington Macauley, *The History of England from the Accession of James II*, 5 vols. (London, 1848), chap. 3.

102. Acosta, *Natural and Moral History of the Indies*, ed. Jane E. Mangan (Durham, N.C., 2002), 244.

103. Léry, *History of a Voyage to the Land of Brazil*, trans. Janet Whately (Berkeley, Calif., 1990), 86–87.

104. On the integration of European livestock and the problems it engendered, see Virginia DeJohn Anderson, "King Philip's Herds: Indians, Colonists, and the Problem of Livestock in Early New England," *William and Mary Quarterly* (hereafter *WMQ*) 3rd ser., 51 (1994), 601–624; idem, Anderson, *Creatures of Empire: How Domestic Animals Transformed Early America* (New York, 2006); Rebecca Kugel, "Of Missionaries and Their Cattle: Ojibwa Perceptions of a Missionary as Evil Shaman," *Ethnohistory* 41 (1994), 226–244; Claudio Saunt, *A New Order of Things: Property, Power, and the Transformation of the Creek Indians, 1733–1816* (New York, 1999).

105. See Krech, *Ecological Indian*, 15–27.

106. Ingeborg Marshall, *A History and Ethnography of the Beothuk* (Montreal and Kingston, 1996), 379.

107. Eduoardo Kohn, *How Forests Think: Toward an Anthropology Beyond the Human* (Berkeley, Calif., 2013), 2.

108. See Kohn, *How Forests Think*, 1–2; Toribio de Ortiguera, "Jornada Del Río Marañón," in Zerrano y Zanz, ed., *Historiadores de Indias*, II (Madrid, 1909), 407–408.

109. See Charles Francis Hall, *Life with the Esquimaux: The Narrative of Captain Charles Francis Hall, of the Whaling Barque "George Henry," from the 29th May, 1860 to the 13th September, 1862*, 2 vols. (London, 1864), 2: 110–111.

110. Marshall, *History and Ethnography of the Beothuk*, 379–380, 390.

111. See Peter C. Mancall, "The Raw and the Cooked: Five Missing Sailors in Sixteenth-Century Nunavut," *WMQ* 3rd ser., 70 (2013), 3–40.

112. The best sources for local conditions in and near Hudson Bay in this period are [Thomas James], *The Strange and Dangerous Voyage of Captain Thomas James* (London, 1633) and Luke Foxe, *North-West Fox, or, Fox from the North-West Passage* (London, 1635).

113. [Bernard], *Cérémonies, moeurs, et coutumes religieuse de tous les peoples du monde*, 7: 88–89.

114. The survivors of the English explorer Henry Hudson's last voyage reported seeing small stone huts with preserved birds hung in them; see Samuel Purchas, *Purchas his Pilgrimes*, 5 vols. (London, 1625), 3: 600.

CHAPTER TWO

1. "Vallard Atlas," HM 29, Huntington Library, f. 12.

2. These illustrations cover the left- and right-hand margins of the first four maps, but only the left margin of the fifth—an image primarily devoted to southern Africa. See HM 29, ff. 1–5, and Carlos Miranda García-Tejedor, "The Mythological Narrative in the Margins of the *Vallard Atlas*," in M. Moliero, ed., *Vallard Atlas* (Barcelona, 2000), 198–215.

3. For the context of the creation of the "Vallard Atlas," see Gayle K. Brunelle, "Images of Empire: Francis I and His Cartographers," in Martin Grosman et al., eds., *Princes and Princely Culture, 1450–1650* (Leiden, 2003), 81–102.

4. HM 29, f. 5; Luís Filipe F. R. Thomaz and Dennis Reinhartz, "The Maps of the Vallard Atlas," in Moleiro, ed., *Vallard Atlas*, 140–141. For Fries, see Laurentius Frisius, *Carta marina universalis 1530* (rpt. Munich, n.d.) (HEH 82668).

5. Hakluyt, *Principal Navigations,* II, ii, 189.

6. "Qu'il était 'de tout temps sorti di cette bonne ville les plus expérimentés capitaines, et pilotes les plus habiles, et les plus hardis navigateurs de l'Europe; que ceux de ce lieu-là avaient fait les premières découvertes des pays les plus élongnés": quoted in Helen Wallis, ed., *The Maps and Text of the Boke of Idrography presented by Jean Rotz to Henry VIII Now in the British Library* (Oxford, 1981), 4.

7. *Boke of Idrography*, 39; G[uillaume] B[rouscon], [world chart], HM 46.

8. Rotz, *Idrography*, 5v–6r; Brouscon; "Vallard Atlas," ff. 3r–4v.

9. Not all ships that ran aground remained there; Hudson's crew refloated the *Discovery* in the spring of 1611 and some of Willem Barentsz's men pieced together craft to get them back home in 1597. See Gerrit de Veer, *Warhafftige Relation: Der Dreyen Newen Unerhörten* (Noribergaie, 1598); Mancall, *Fatal Journey,*

10. Rotz, *Boke of Idrography*, ff. 14r, 15v–16r, 17v–18r, 22r.

11. "The new fonde Londe wuhaz men goeth a fishing": *Boke of Idrography*, ff. 23v–24r.

12. Rotz, *Boke of Idrography*, ff. 26r, 28r.

13. Surekha Davies, "Depictions of Brazilians on French Maps, 1542–1555," *Historical Journal* 55 (2012), 317–318.

14. Luís Filipe F. R. Thomaz, "The *Vallard Atlas* and Sixteenth Century Knowledge of Australia," in Moleiro, ed., *Vallard Atlas*, 28–82.

15. While it is difficult to measure the visual pleasures that any image produces, the repeated use of the "Vallard" in illustrations provides a hint of its modern-day value. A detail, for example, is on the cover illustration of the *Historical Atlas of Canada: Canada's History Illustrated with Original Maps*

(Seattle, Wash., 2002), and another adorns the cover of Davies, *Renaissance Ethnography*.

16. "Vallard Atlas," f. 11. Over the course of the sixteenth century, Europeans substituted brazilwood and cochineal for earlier sources of red dye, which they had previously found in south Asia and the southwest Pacific. See R. A. Donkin, "Spanish Red: An Ethnogeographical Study of Cochineal and the Opuntia Cactus," *Transactions of the American Philosophical Society*, n.s. 67 (1977), 1–84, and J. H. Holland, "Brazil-Wood," *Bulletin of Miscellaneous Information (Royal Gardens, Kew)* 9 (1916), 209–225; for beaver pelts, see Eric Wolfe, *Europe and the People Without History*, 2nd ed. (Berkeley, 2010), 158–160. The Portuguese recognized the value of brazilwood, which was crucial to the Iberian empire's finances well before the rise of the region's other notable exports—gold, sugar, and tobacco; by the early seventeenth century, the king's own treasurer had administrative control over these trees' export. See Robert C. Smith, "The Wood-Beach at Recife: A Contribution to the Economic History of Brazil," *Americas* 6 (1949), 209–233, esp. 215 and 224. But the trade eventually faded with the spread of sugar plantations. As the environmental historian John R. McNeill put it, "What dyewood cutters left standing...sugar planters would soon burn." See McNeill, "Agriculture, Forests, and Ecological History: Brazil, 1500–1984," *Environmental History* 10 (1986), 123–133, quotation at 124.

17. See C. R. Boxer, ed., *The Tragic History of the Sea, 1589–1622*, Hakluyt Society, 2nd ser., 112 (Cambridge, Eng., 1959).

18. Alfredo Pinheiro Marque, Luís Filipe F. R. Thomaz, and Bernardo Sá Nogueira, "Geographical and Toponymic Study of the Regional Charts in the *Atlas Miller*," in Manuel Moliero, ed., *Atlas Miller* (Barcelona, 2006), 344–345.

19. See Jennifer L. Anderson, *Mahogany: The Costs of Luxury in Early America* (Cambridge, Mass., 2012); Michael Williams, *Americans and Their Forests: A Historical Geography* (Cambridge, Eng., 1989), 53–110; [Arthur Standish], *The Commons Complaint* (London, 1611); William Strachey, *Historie of Travaile into Virginia Britannia*, ed. Louis B. Wright and Virginia Freund, Hakluyt Society, 2nd ser., 103 (London, 1953), 130; Andrew McRae, "Tree-Felling in Early Modern England: Michael Drayton's Environmentalism," *Review of English Studies*, n.s. 63 (2011), 410–430; P. Warde, "Fear of Wood Shortage and the Reality of the Woodland in Europe, c. 1450–1850," *History Workshop Journal* 62 (2006), 28–57; Robert G. Albion, *Forests and Sea Power: The Timber Problem of the Royal Navy, 1652–1862* (Cambridge, Mass., 1926), 95–138, 280; McNeill, "Agriculture, Forests, and Ecological History," 124–125. By the sixteenth century, some Europeans fretted over depleted forests despite long-existing practices of forest management. Venetians, who inhabited a city dependent on wood for normal kinds of construction and fuel, had an espe-

cially pressing need for wood, which they relied on for the pilings to keep their houses afloat in the lagoon and also to construct the ships necessary for their commerce. But despite some public concerns about declines in supply, managerial policies in place dating to the fourteenth century prevented crises relating to a lack of wood through the sixteenth century and well beyond. See Karl Appuhn, *A Forest on the Sea: Environmental Expertise in Renaissance Venice* (Baltimore, 2009).

20. Alfred W. Crosby, *Ecological Imperialism: The Biological Expansion of Europe, 900–1900* (Cambridge, Eng., 1986), 145–170.

21. On fresh water available on icebergs, see the literature on brine extrusion: R. A. Lake and E. L. Lewis, "Salt Rejection by Sea Ice During Growth," *Journal of Geophysical Research* 75 (1970), 583–597, and W. S. Reeburgh, "Fluxes Associated with Brine Motion in Growing Sea Ice," *Polar Biology* 3 (1984), 29–33.

22. "Vallard Atlas," f. 9, f. 12.

23. Europeans left most surviving maps from the sixteenth-century Atlantic basin, but those from the hands of Native Americans reveal different visual agendas from those typically found produced by newcomers to the Western Hemisphere. See Barbara E. Mundy, *The Mapping of New Spain: Indigenous Cartography and the Maps of the Relaciones Geográficas* (Chicago, 1996).

24. On beaver ecology, see Morrell Allred, *Beaver Behavior* (Happy Camp, Calif., 1986); John Bishir, Richard Lancia, and Harry Hodgdon, "Beaver Family Organization: Its Implications for Colony Size," in G. Pilleri, ed., *Investigations on Beavers* (Berne, Switzerland, 1986), 105–113.

25. The best recent study, which reveals in depth how the fur trade evolved in the Canadian north, is Ann M. Carlos and Frank D. Lewis, *Commerce by a Frozen Sea: Native Americans and the European Fur Trade* (Philadelphia, 2010).

26. "Vallard Atlas," f. 1.

27. "Vallard Atlas," f. 8; Thomas and Reinhartz, "Maps of the *Vallard Atlas*," 166–174.

28. "Vallard Atlas," f. 4; Thomas and Reinhartz, "Maps of the *Vallard Atlas*," 134–138.

29. "Vallard Atlas," f. 7.

30. E.g., "Iselandia" for Iceland, "Norovaga" for Norway, "Irlandia" for Ireland; "Vallard Atlas," f. 8.

31. "Vallard Atlas," f. 8.

32. See Crosby, *Columbian Exchange*; idem, *Ecological Imperialism*; David Jones, "Virgin Soils Revisited," *WMQ*, 3rd ser., 60 (2004), 703–742; idem, *Rationalizing Epidemics: Meanings and Uses of American Indian Mortality Since 1600* (Cambridge, Mass., 2004).

33. See Martin, *Keepers of the Game*; Adrian Tanner, *Bringing Home Animals*; Shepherd Krech III, ed., *Indians, Animals, and the Fur Trade: A Critique of Keepers of the Game* (Athens, Ga., 1981).

34. Thomas Harriot, *The Briefe and True Report of the Newfound Land of Virginia* (Frankfurt-am-Main, 1590), 29; Joyce Chaplin, *Subject Matter: Technology, The Body, and Science on the Anglo-American Frontier, 1500–1676* (Cambridge, Mass., 2001), 28–34.

35. See, e.g., William Bradford, *Of Plymouth Plantation*, ed. Samuel Eliot Morrison (New York, 1951), 270–271.

36. Arthur J. O. Anderson, "Sahagún's Prologues and Interpolations," in Bernardino de Sahagún, *Florentine Codex: General History of the Things of New Spain*, part 1, *Introduction and Indices*, 94; Kerpel, *Colors of the New World*, 14.

37. John L. Brooke, *Climate Change and the Course of Global History: A Rough Journey* (New York, 2014), 431–432; Jones, "Virgin Soils Revisited," 703–742; James Axtell, "Native Reactions to the Invasion of America," in Axtell, *Natives and Newcomers: The Cultural Origins of North America* (New York, 2001), 299. As Brooke notes, in the case of the 1570s epidemic, it is possible that a drought made the infection more dangerous because of an expansion in the rodent population following the return of rainfall. See Brooke, *Climate Change*, 439–440.

38. Columbus, *Barcelona Letter*, 65, 68.

39. See Amy Buono, "'Their Treasures Are the Feathers of Birds': Tupinambá Featherwork and the Image of America," in Alessandra Russo, Gerhard Wolf, and Diana Fane, eds., *Images Take Flight: Feather Art in Mexico and Europe* (Florence and Mexico City, 2015), 178–189.

40. Léry, *Voyage to the Land of Brazil*, 15; de Bry, *Americae Tertia Pars* (Frankfurt, 1592), 151.

41. Hakluyt, *A Particuler Discourse Concerninge the Greate Necessitie and Manifolde Commodyties that are like to growe to this Realme of Englande by the Western Discoveries lately attempted . . . Known as Discourse of Western Planting* [1584], ed. David B. Quinn and Alison M. Quinn, Hakluyt Society, extra ser., 45 (London, 1993), 16–27, 115–116.

42. See, e.g., J. B. Harley, *The New Nature of Maps* (Baltimore, 2001).

43. Thomas and Reinhartz, "Maps of the *Vallard Atlas*," 97.

44. "Vallard Atlas," f. 6.

45. See Dava Sobel, *Longitude* (New York, 2007).

46. For Europeans' obsession about wind patterns, see Alessandro Nova, *The Book of the Wind: The Representation of the Invisible* (Montreal and Kingston, 2011).

47. See Arthur Thibert, *Eskimo (Inuktitut) Dictionary*, rev. ed. (New York,

2004), 52, 64. The anthropologist Franz Boas's limited list of Inuktitut words from Baffin Island includes those for different kinds of winds, revealing long-term persistence of the significance of such terms; see Ludger Müller-Wille, ed., *Franz Boas Among the Inuit of Baffin Island, 1883–1884: Journals and Letters*, trans. William Barr (Toronto, 1998), 273–276.

48. The American sea captain Charles Francis Hall reported a 200-year-old incident in which Inuit claimed they had sung for five stranded English sailors eager to get home; see Hall, *Life with the Esquimaux: The Narrative of Captain Charles Francis Hall, of the Whaling Barque "George Henry," from the 29th May, 1860, to the 13th September, 1862*, 2 vols. (London, 1864), 2: 284. For Mesoamerica, see Stuart B. Schwartz, *Sea of Storms: A History of Hurricanes in the Greater Caribbean from Columbus to Katrina* (Princeton, N.J., 2015), 5–9, quotation at 8.

49. Magnus, *Description of the Northern Peoples*, I: 173.

50. "Vallard Atlas," ff. 13–15; Thomas and Reinhartz, "Maps of the *Vallard Atlas*," 187–195.

51. For a treatment of this image in its context, see David Harris Sacks, "Discourses of Western Planting: Richard Hakluyt and the Making of the Atlantic World," in Mancall, ed., *Atlantic World and Virginia*, 444–446.

52. *Magellan's Voyage: A Narrative Account of the First Circumnavigation*, trans. and ed. R. A. Skelton (New Haven, Conn., 1969), 46–50.

53. See, e.g., the depiction of what is presumably Venice on f. 14, identifiable by both San Marco and the tower in the piazza.

54. See Judith A. Carney, *Black Rice: The African Origins of Rice Cultivation in the Americas* (Cambridge, Mass., 2001), 73–76.

55. Jean de Léry, *History of a Voyage to the Land of Brazil*, trans. Janet Whatley (Berkeley, Calif., 1990), 164.

56. "Vallard Atlas," f. 8 (Iceland) and f. 9 (Labrador and Newfoundland).

57. See, e.g., Cronon, *Changes in the Land*, 34–53.

58. See Maryanne Kowaleski, "The Expansion of the South-Western Fisheries in Late Medieval England," *Economic History Review* 53 (2000), 429–454, and W. Jeffrey Bolster, *The Mortal Sea: Fishing the Atlantic in the Age of Sail* (Cambridge, Mass., 2012), 12–48.

59. Hakluyt, for one, recognized the speciousness of the claim, which he attacked in his "Discourse"; see *Discourse on Western Planting*, ed. Quinn and Quinn, 96–112.

60. "Vallard Atlas," f. 6v.

61. The best description is in Verlyn Klinkenborg's introduction to the facsimile edition, published as *The Drake Manuscript in the Pierpont Morgan Library: Histoire Naturelle des Indes* (London, 1996), xv–xxii. All references below, unless otherwise indicated, are from the manuscript at the Morgan, but I have used the translations from the facsimile, found on 253–272.

62. See Nancy G. Siraisi, *Medieval and Early Renaissance Medicine: An Introduction to Knowledge and Practice* (Chicago, 1990).

63. For the later development of modes of description for American plants, see in particular Daniela Bleichmar, *Visible Empire: Botanic Expeditions and Visual Culture in the Hispanic Enlightenment* (Chicago, 2012).

64. "Histoire Naturelle," f. 2 (garlic), f. 4 (pineapple), f. 5v (squash), f. 10v (sweet potato).

65. The most extensive work on the early history of tobacco is Jerome E. Brooks, *Tobacco: Its History Illustrated by the Books, Manuscripts and Engravings of the Library of George Arents, Jr.*, 5 vols. (New York, 1937–1952); see also Mancall, "Tales Tobacco Told," 648–678.

66. "Histoire Naturelle," f. 4v.

67. "Histoire Naturelle," f. 92.

68. *A Counterblaste to Tobacco* (London, 1604) was the first published work of James VI of Scotland—who became James I of England in 1603.

69. "Histoire Naturelle," f. 99 (gold), f. 120 (fishing), f. 119 (cotton), ff. 83 and 88 (parrots), f. 57 (pearl diving); on the obsession for pearls, see Molly A. Warsh, "A Political Ecology in the Early Spanish Caribbean," *WMQ* 3rd ser., 71 (2014), 517–548.

70. "Histoire Naturelle," f. 78 (firefly); for manatees hauling people across water, see Pietro Martire d'Anghiera, *The Decades of the Newe World*, trans. Richard Eden (London, 1555), 130–131.

71. "Vallard Atlas," HM 29, f. 12; "Atlas nautique du monde; dit Atlas Miller," Bibliotheque Nationale. On Tupinambá featherwork, see Buono, "'Their Treasures Are the Feathers of Birds,'" 178–189.

72. "Histoire Naturelle," f. 104 (African laborers), f. 91 (wheat trade).

73. "Histoire Naturelle," ff. 93v–94r [uninhabited island], f. 72 (mosquitoes).

74. See "The Strange and Dangerous Voyage of Captain Thomas James," in M. Christy, ed., *The Voyages of Captain Luke Foxe of Hull, and Captain Thomas James of Bristol . . . in 1631–32*, 2 vols., Hakluyt Society, 1st ser., vols. 88–89 (London, 1893–1894), II: 562–563.

75. Amy J. Buono, "Representing the Tupinambá and the Brazilwood Trade in Sixteenth-Century Rouen," in Regina R. Félix and Scott D. Juall, eds., *Cultural Exchanges Between Brazil and France* (West Lafayette, Ind., 2016), 19–34; Michael Wintroub, *A Savage Mirror: Power, Identity, and Knowledge in Early Modern France* (Stanford, Calif., 2006).

CHAPTER THREE

1. For one group's intellectual maps, see Renée Fossett, "Mapping Inuktut: Inuit Views of the Real World," in Jennifer S. H. Brown and Elizabeth Vibert,

eds., *Reading Beyond Words: Contexts for Native History*, 2nd ed. (Toronto, 2009), 111–131.

2. Columbus, "Barcelona Letter," 65.

3. Winthrop, "Reasons to Be Considered for Justifying the Undertakers of the Intended Plantation in New England . . . ," Massachussetts Historical Society *Proceedings* 8 (1864–1865), 420–425.

4. Cronon, *Changes in the Land*, 54–81.

5. For the variety of strategies, see Patricia Seed, *Ceremonies of Possession in Europe's Conquest of the New World, 1492–1640* (Cambridge, Eng., 1995).

6. See, e.g., Hernán Cortés, *Letters from Mexico*, trans. Anthony Pagden (New Haven, Conn., 1986), 102–112. Ramusio did not do much more, although he did include a picture of Hochelaga; see *Terze Volume de Navigationi et Viaggi* (Venice, 1556), 446v–447r.

7. Hugo Grotius, *Mare Liberum* [1609], translated at some point between 1609 and 1616 by Richard Hakluyt as *The Free Sea*, ed. David Armitage (Indianapolis, Ind., 2004). For Dee, see Cotton Augustus I i, British Library and David Armitage, *The Ideological Origins of the British Empire* (Cambridge, Eng., 2000), 47.

8. Ro[bert] Fotherby, "A Voyage of Discoverie to Greenland, & c.," in *Purchas his Pilgrimes*, III: 722; "Strange and dangerous voyage of Captain Thomas James," 565.

9. See Peter C. Mancall, "'Collecting Americans': The Anglo-American Experience from Cabot to NAGPRA," in Daniela Bleichmar and Peter C. Mancall, eds., *Collecting Across Cultures: Material Exchanges in the Early Modern Atlantic World* (Philadelphia, 2011), 192–213.

10. See [Robert Fabian], *The Great Chronicle of London (Guildhall MS 3313)*, ed. A. H. Thomas and E. D. Thornley (London, 1938), 320. Richard Hakluyt and John Stow both used this source when they retold the story; see Hakluyt, *Divers voyages touching the discoverie of America and the Ilands adjacent* (London, 1582), sig. A3r–v, and Stow, *The Chronicles of England, from Brute unto this present yeare of Christ, 1580* (London, [1580]), 875. The chronology of this early capture is uncertain because of ambiguities relating to the explorations of the Cabots; see Alden Vaughan, *Transatlantic Encounters: American Indians in Britain, 1500–1776* (Cambridge, Eng., 2006), 11.

11. [George Best], *A True Discourse of the late voyages of discoverie, for the finding of a passage to Cathaya, by the Northwest, under the conduct of Martin Frobisher Generall* (London, 1578), 16.

12. Michael Gaudio, *Engraving the Savage: The New World and Techniques of Civilization* (Minneapolis, 2008); Paul Hulton and David B. Quinn, *American Drawings of John White, 1577–1590*, 2 vols. (Chapel Hill, 1964), 6–11; Hugh Honour, *The New Golden Land: European Images of America from the Discoveries to the Present Time* (New York, 1975), 68–78.

13. See, e.g., Bruce R. Smith, "Mouthpieces: Native American Voices in Thomas Harriot's 'True and Brief Report of . . . Virginia,' Gaspar Pérez De Villagrá's 'Historia de la Nuevo México,' and John Smith's 'General History of Virginia,'" *New Literary History* 32 (2001), 501–517; Mary C. Fuller, *Voyages in Print: English Travels to America, 1576–1624* (Cambridge, Eng., 1995); John Bakeless, *The Eyes of Discovery: America as Seen by Its First Explorers* (orig. pub. 1950; rpt. New York, 1989), 176–196; Joan Pau Rubiés, "Travel Writing and Ethnography," in Peter Hulme and Tim Youngs, eds., *The Cambridge Companion to Travel Writing* (Cambridge, Eng., 2002), 242–260.

14. Charles B. Heiser Jr., "The Sunflower Among the North American Indians," *Proceedings of the American Philosophical Society* 95 (1951), 433–435; Daniel W. Gade, "Shifting Synanthropy of the Crow in Eastern North America," *Geographical Review* 100 (2010), 152.

15. Kim Sloan, *A New World: England's First View of America* (Chapel Hill, N.C., 2007), 11–12.

16. Michiel van Groesen, *The Representations of the Overseas World in the de Bry Collection of Voyages (1590–1634)* (Leiden, 2008); Karen Ordahl Kupperman, *Indians and English: Facing Off in Early America* (Ithaca, 2000), 143–146; Mancall, *Hakluyt's Promise*, 196–207; Richter, *Before the Revolution*, 110–111; David Beers Quinn, ed., *The Roanoke Voyages, 1584–1590*, 2 vols., Hakluyt Society, 2nd ser., 104–105 (London, 1955), I: 390–464; Chaplin, *Subject Matter*, 28–34.

17. See, e.g., the use of these images in U.S. history textbooks: Peter Charles Hoffer, *The Brave New World: A History of Early America* (Boston, 2000), 41; Richard Middleton, *Colonial America: A History, 1565–1776*, 3rd ed. (Malden, Mass., 2002), 10, 32–36; Maria Montoya et al., *Global Americans: A History of the United States* (Boston, 2018), 52, 55.

18. For details about these expeditions and their consequences, see Hakluyt, *Principall Navigations*, 615–635 (Nunavut), 674–700 (Newfoundland).

19. Hakluyt, *Principall Navigations*, 728–773; Mancall, *Hakluyt's Promise*, *passim*.

20. Barlowe and Amadas, "First Voyage made to the coastes of America," in Hakluyt, *Principall Navigations*, 731. Jeremy Belknap picked up this portion, without commentary, two hundred years later; *American Biography*, 2 vols. [Boston 1794–1798; Boston, 1843], I: 304. As David Beers Quinn recognized, Hakluyt actually dropped the last sentence of this section when he reprinted the Barlowe and Amadas report in 1600; see Quinn, ed., *Roanoke Voyages*, I: 108.

21. Engravings of cannibals had circulated well before; see, e.g., Hans Staden, *Warhaftige Historia und Beschreibung eyner Landtschafft der wilden, nacket, grimmigen Menschfresser Leuthen in der Newenwelt America gelege* (Marburg, 1557). In the 1590s, these images recirculated most vividly in de Bry's *Americae*

Tertia pars (Frankfurt, 1592), which included six images of cannibalism in addition to a title page that featured Brazilians eating parts of human bodies.

22. As the historian Sabine MacCormack put it, European explorers "integrated what was new and strange about America into a context of what was familiar and known." See MacCormack, "Limits of Understanding: Perceptions of Greco-Roman and Amerindian Paganism in Early Modern Europe," in Karen Ordahl Kupperman, ed., *America in European Consciousness, 1493–1750* (Chapel Hill, N.C., 1995), 79–80. On the reliance of analogous reasoning in the context of Europeans trying to understand the Western Hemisphere, see also J. H. Elliott, *The Old World and the New, 1482–1650* (Cambridge, Eng., 1970), 40–41; Anthony Pagden, *The Fall of Natural Man: The American Indian and the Origins of Comparative Ethnology* (Cambridge, Eng., 1982), 1–4; Peter C. Mancall, ed., *Travel Narratives from the Age of Discovery* (New York, 2006), 10–13; and Grafton, *New Worlds, Ancient Texts*, esp. 1–10.

23. The instructions were apparently written in 1582 for the painter and surveyor Thomas Blavin, who was to accompany Sir Humphrey Gilbert to Newfoundland; see Hulton and Quinn, *Drawings of John White*, I: 34–35 (citing Add. Mss. 38823, ff. 1–8, British Library); the full text is reproduced in David B. Quinn, ed., *New American World* (New York, 1979), III: 240. The problem of preserving American specimens for voyages back to England baffled travelers for generations; see Bonnie Stadelman, "Flora and Fauna Versus Mice and Mold," *WMQ* 3rd ser., 28 (1971), 595–606.

24. On the history of the drawings and paintings, see Hulton and Quinn, *American Drawings of John White*, 24–27, and Gaudio, *Engraving the Savage*.

25. The most thorough account of the creation and circulation of the images can be found in van Groesen, *The Representations of the Overseas World in the de Bry Collection of Voyages*.

26. For the long-term significance of these images in European understandings of American morbidity and mortality, see Peter C. Mancall, "Illness and Death Among Americans in Bernard Picart's *Cérémonies et Coutumes Religieuses*," in Lynn Hunt, Margaret Jacob, and Wijnand Mijnhardt, eds., *Bernard Picart and the First Global Vision of Religion*, Getty Research Institute Issues and Debates (Los Angeles, 2010), 271–287.

27. Harriot, *Briefe and True Report*, 25.

28. Harriot, *Briefe and True Report*, 26–27.

29. Harriot, *Briefe and True Report*, 25 ("great God"), 26 (men rising from the dead), 29 (conceptions of the English and explanation of physicians' claims).

30. Harriot, *Briefe and True Report*, 29.

31. Harriot, *Briefe and True Report*, 29. For one contemporary's view of the multiple causes of illness, see T[homas] B[rasbridge], *The Poor mans Jewell, that is to say, a treatise of the Pestilence* (London, 1578).

32. Hakluyt was among the scholars working to get the 1590 edition moving forward; see van Groesen, *Representations of the Overseas World* , 112–116, and Mancall, *Hakluyt's Promise*, 196–209.

33. The pictures can be found in Hulton and Quinn, *American Drawings of John White*, II, plates 2 and 3 (Puerto Rico), plates 4–30, 49–57 (specimens).

34. Hulton and Quinn, *American Drawings of John White*, II, plate 32; Harriot, *Briefe and True Report*, plate VIII.

35. Hulton and Quinn, *American Drawings of John White*, II, plates 37 and 35; Harriot, *Briefe and True Report*, plate XXII.

36. Hulton and Quinn, *American Drawings of John White*, II, plate 42; Harriot, *Briefe and True Report*, plate XIII.

37. See Hulton and Quinn, *American Drawings of John White*, II, plate 35.

38. On the myriad ways that Algonquian and Iroquoian peoples stored and used maize, see Betty Fussell, *The Story of Corn* (New York, 2004), and Arthur C. Parker, *Iroquois Uses of Maize and Other Food Plants* (Albany, N.Y., 1910).

39. See, e.g., Reginald Scot, *A Perfite platforme of a Hoppe Garden* (London, 1576), 11–14; see also Conrad Heresbach, *Foure Bookes of Husbandrie* (London, 1586), 52. Scot, who included illustrations in his book, believed that the information he conveyed about planting needed to extend beyond the literate. As he put it, "I desire of the learned patience in reading, of the unlearned, diligence in hearing" (sig. Biir). In a later edition, Scot noted that "grounde orderly used, doth not onely yeelde the more, the greater, the harder, and the weyghtyer hopes, but also they shall goe further, they shall endure longer, they shall be holesomer for the body, and pleasanter of verdure or taste, than such as be disorderly handled." See Reynolde Scot, *A Perfite platform of a Hoppe Garden* (London, 1578), 5.

40. Hulton and Quinn, *American Drawings of John White*, II, plate 58.

41. Cf. van Groesen, *Representations of the Overseas World*, 139, and Sacks, "Discourses of Western Planting," 410–453.

42. Kupperman, *Indians and English*, 79.

43. All details here and in the following two paragraphs are from Harriot, *Briefe and True Report*, 25–27.

44. Harriot, *Briefe and True Report*, 26.

45. Harriot, *Briefe and True Report*, 27.

46. Harriot, *Briefe and True Report*, 28.

47. Bolton, *The Elements of Armories* (London, 1610), 20–22.

48. Purchas, *Purchas his Pilgrimmage* (London, 1613), 637–638.

49. Wooldridge, "Indians of Virginia" (c. 1675), Crystal Bridges Museum of American Art, Bentonville, Ark. (2006.10).

50. Chatelain, *Carte pour l'Introduction a l'Histoire d'Angleterre ou l'on Voit son Premier Gouvernement et l'Etat Abrege de cette Monarchie sous les Empereur Romains et sou les Rois Saxons* (Amsterdam, 1720).

51. Beverley, *History and Present State of Virginia* (London, 1705), Book III, opp. 3 (tattoos), opp. 6 (priest), opp. 7 (women), opp. 31 (Kiwasa), opp. 48 (ossuary); [Bernard], *Cérémonies, moeurs, et coutumes réligieuses de tous les peuples du monde*, 7 vols. (Paris, 1741), 7: opp. 114 (Kiwasa), opp. 116 (priest), opp. 122 (ossuary).

52. Sir William Keith, *The History of the British Plantations in America* (London, 1738), 39–41, ff.

53. William Oldys, *The Life of Sir Walter Ralegh* ([London?, 1736?]), included in an edition of Sir Walter Ralegh, *The Historie of the World* (London, 1671), xxxiii–xxxiv.

54. William Stith, *The History of the First Discovery and Settlement of Virginia* (London, 1753), 11.

55. Stith, *History of the First Discovery*, 16–17.

56. Belknap, *American Biography*, I: 304.

57. Jefferson to Adams, June 11, 1812, in Lester Cappon, ed., *The Adams-Jefferson Letters; The Complete Correspondence Between Thomas Jefferson and Abigail and John Adams* (Chapel Hill, N.C., 2012), 305–306; Gaudio, *Engraving the Savage*, xiii.

58. See, e.g., *La navigation du capitaine Martin Forbisher* (La Rochelle, 1578); *Beschreibung der Shiffart des Haubtmans Martine Forbissher* (Nuremberg, 1580); D. Joan. Tho. Freigium, *De Martini Forbisseri Angli navigatione in regiones occidentis et septentrionis narratio historica* (Noribergae, 1580).

59. *Graphic Sketches from Old and Authentic Works, Illustrating the Costume, Habits and Character of the Aborigines of America* (New York, 1841), 1.

POSTSCRIPT

1. Moffet's work competed with a study by the Bologna-based physician Ulisse Aldrovandi, whose *De Animalubis insectus* had been published in 1602. For a superb study of the two texts and their sources, see Janice Neri, *The Insect and the Image: Visualizing Nature in Early Modern Europe, 1500–1700* (Minneapolis, Minn., 2011), 27–73.

2. The original has been in the collection of the J. Paul Getty Museum since 1986; for a facsimile, see Lee Hendrix and Thea Vignau-Wilberg, *Mir Calligraphiae Monumenta: A Sixteenth-Century Calligraphic Manuscript Inscribed by Georg Bocskay and Illuminated by Joris Hoefnagel* (Malibu, 1992).

3. Neri, *Insect and the Image*, 45–60; see also Katherine Acheston, "Gesner, Topsell, and the Purposes of Pictures in Early Modern Natural Histories," in Michael Hunter, ed., *Printed Images in Early Modern Britain: Essays in Interpretation* (London, 2010), 127–144.

4. For the larger European intellectual context of scholars wrestling with how to prove the authority of their texts by drawing explicitly on those who

came before, see Anthony Grafton, *The Footnote: A Curious History* (Cambridge, Mass., 1997), 125–147.

5. On Sahagún's approach and purpose, see Alfredo López Austin, "The Research Method of Fray Bernardino de Sahagún: The Questionnaires," in Munro S. Edmonson, ed., *Sixteenth-Century Mexico: The Work of Sahagún* (Albuquerque, N.M., 1974), 111–149, esp. 112–120.

6. Kerpel, *Colors of the New World*, 2–3, 7, 21, quotation at 3.

7. The idea of bees and the maintenance of the hive served as models for colonization long before Mandeville wrote; see Karen Ordahl Kupperman, "The Beehive as a Model for Colonial Design," in Kupperman, ed., *America in European Consciousness*, 272–292.

8. The English edition was the product of the surgeon George Baker and the book collector Thomas Hill, who was also the possible translator. They dedicated the work to William Paddy, the king's physician, and to the French physician Theodore Mayerne, who had been responsible for the publication of the Latin edition of the work in 1634 but who had died in 1655. For the details of this part of the work's publishing history, see Neri, *Insect and the Image*, 61–62.

9. Moffet, *Theatre of Insects*, sig. Ffff3r.

10. Moffet, *Theatre of Insects*, sig. Ffff3r.

11. Moffet, *Theatre of Insects*, sig. Ffffv.

12. Moffet, *Theatre of Insects*, sig. Ffff3v.

13. Moffet, *Theatre of Insects*, sig. [Ffff4r].

14. Moffet, *Theatre of Insects*, sig. [Ffff4r].

15. Moffet, *Theatre of Insects*, sig. [Ffff4v].

16. Moffet, *Theatre of Insects*, sig. [Ffff5r].

17. Moffet, *Theatre of Insects*, sig. [Ffff5v].

18. Moffet, *Theatre of Insects*, sig. [Ffff5v].

19. Moffet, *Theatre of Insects*, sig. [Ffff6r].

20. Moffet, *Theatre of Insects*, sig. [Ffff6v].

21. Moffet, *Theatre of Insects*, [1029; numbered incorrectly in text as 1149].

22. Moffet, *Theatre of Insects*, 980.

23. Moffet, *Theatre of Insects*, 889. On laws, see, e.g., the *Bechbretha* (the Bee Laws), likely codified in seventh-century Ireland, which specified what happened when bees took up residence on new lands (they became the property of the landowner), the kinds of pledges that a beekeeper needed to make to neighbors, and what happened when one's bees blinded another (the victim in one known case received a hive as compensation). See Thomas Charles-Edwards and Fergus Kelly, trans., *Bechbretha: [an old Irish law-tract on bee-keeping]* (Dublin, 1983), and Fergus Kelly, *A Guide to Early Irish Law* (Dublin, 1988), 124, 165–166, 239.

24. Moffet, *Theatre of Insects*, 892.

25. Moffet, *Theatre of Insects*, 894.

26. Moffet, *Theatre of Insects*, 923, 921.

27. Moffet, *Theatre of Insects*, 894.

28. Moffet, *Theatre of Insects*, 895.

29. Moffet, *Theatre of Insects*, 895–896.

30. Moffet, *Theatre of Insects*, 905.

31. Moffet, *Theatre of Insects*, 927.

32. Moffet, *Theatre of Insects*, 907.

33. Moffet, *Theatre of Insects*, 911–914.

34. As the historian of science James Raven argued, Moffet drew on multiple sources, especially the work of Thomas Penny, but the book on insects represented a major contribution to European understanding of the natural world. See Raven, *English Naturalists from Neckham to Ray: A Study of the Making of the Modern World* (Cambridge, Eng., 1947), 172–191.

35. It is also possible that the English-language editor of Moffet's book relied, at least in this section, on Topsell's work, which was his last major publication and was known well enough to solidify his place among a community of early modern European natural historians, a point he made in the beginning of what would have been his next book—which he never finished—on the natural history of birds. See Topsell's "The Fowles of Heaven; or History of Birdes," EL 1142, HEH. On Topsell as having access to Moffet's work and as a likely plagiarist, see Raven, *English Naturalists*, 180, 223–224.

36. Topsell, *Historie of Serpents*, 64 ("cut-wasted creatures"), 246–276 (spiders), 306–315 (earthworms), 64–82 (bees), 83–92 (wasps), 92–96 (hornets), 102–111 (caterpillars).

37. *Florentine Codex*, 11: 97.

38. *Florentine Codex*, 11: 96.

39. *Florentine Codex*, 11: 89–91.

40. *Florentine Codex*, 11: 92.

41. *Florentine Codex*, 11: 93.

42. *Florentine Codex*, 11: 92.

43. *Florentine Codex*, 11: 99.

44. *Florentine Codex*, 11: 100–101.

45. *Florentine Codex*," 11: 122 and 180 (on the *nopal*), 239–240 (on cochineal).

46. For the larger quest, see, among others, Elena Phipps, *Cochineal Red: The Art History of a Color* (New York, 2012).

47. The Spanish scholar José de Acosta, who was more interested in the animals, plants, minerals, and rituals of the peoples of New Spain, wrote about

cochineal and even offered an estimate of its annual value—283,750 pesos. See Acosta, *Natural and Moral History*, 213.

48. *Florentine Codex*, 11: 240–245. For a modern analysis of this color mixing, see Kerpel, *Colors of the New World*, 21–25.

49. Léry, *History of a Voyage,* 92–94. Léry, it should be noted, saw himself as part of an international discussion about nature; in his section on insects, he referred repeatedly to the Spanish historian Francisco López de Gómara's writings about New Spain. For the circulation of Léry's text, see *History of a Voyage*, trans. Whately, 257–259.

NOTE ON SOURCES

1. William Bartram, *Travels Through North & South Carolina, Georgia, East & West Florida* (Philadelphia, 1791), [xiii].

2. Timothy Dwight, *Travels; in New-England and New-York*, 4 vols. (New Haven, Conn., 1821), 1: 9.

3. I have written about the extent and process of discovery elsewhere; see Mancall, "The Age of Discovery," *Reviews in American History* 26 (1998), 26–53.

4. For a more general assessment of the available literature for the early modern era, see Mancall, "Pigs for Historians: *Changes in the Land* and Beyond," *WMQ* 3rd ser., 67 (2010), 347–375.

5. George P. Marsh, *Man and Nature: Or, Physical Geography as Modified by Human Action*, ed. David Lowenthal (orig. pub. New York, 1864; Seattle, Wash., 2003), quotations at 119, 4, and 36.

INDEX

Waldseemüller, Martin, 45, 47
Walker, B. N. O. (Wyandot), 28–29
Walsingham, Sir Francis, 101, 112
wheat, 81
White, John, 88, 92, 95, 112–13, 119,
    plates 10–11; paintings of, altered by
    de Bry engravings, 88–89, 93–94,
    96–97, 96f–99f, 100–101, 102f, 103f.
    See also *The Briefe and True Report of*
    the Newfound Land of Virginia (1590)

wind: patterns of, 63, 72f; lore of, 25,
    65–66
Winthrop, John, 86
wonders. *See* monsters
Wooldridge, James, 109
Worster, Donald, xiii, 141
Wotton, Edward, 123
Wyandot, 28–29

Yuchi, 30

ACKNOWLEDGMENTS

I walked into the church at Fréjus on a hot summer day in 2004 and realized that I wanted to write about the fourteenth-century paintings that decorated the wooden cloister. Here was a series of visual images of an entire physical world, a chaotic blend of nature and culture staring down at modern viewers from medieval rafters. From that moment this short book began to take shape, although my ideas were as disorganized as those ancient wooden panels. I wanted to set those faded portraits of monks and monsters into an interpretation of the early modern Atlantic basin. Figuring out the context took more time than I could have imagined, and it would never have occurred without the (possibly divinely inspired) intervention of many individuals and institutions. I am very pleased to finally thank them in print.

This book in its present form began as the Mellon Distinguished Lectures in the Humanities, which I delivered at the McNeil Center at the University of Pennsylvania. I thank Bob Lockhart for the invitation, as well as my other friends at the Press, notably Peter Agree and Director Eric Halpern. I want to also thank Dan Richter, who gracefully hosted the lectures at the McNeil Center, and Jeff Kallberg, who managed the grant that made these lectures possible. The McNeil Center is one of the great stars in the firmament of humanities centers, and the audiences for those lectures provided the kind of stimulating feedback that every scholar wants—including one especially perceptive sophomore who asked the kind of brilliant question that I have known him to speak since I first met him in 1992.

I wrote this book at the Huntington Library, and for support there I thank Roy Ritchie, the former research director, and Steve Hindle, his successor. In the time since those initial lectures I have had an opportunity to present parts of this book at a series of venues, and I am delighted to now thank my hosts: Mark Peterson and his colleagues in the history department at Berkeley (with special guest Saul Perlmutter), Sophie LeMercier-Godard at the École Normale Supérieure de Lyon, Neil Safier at the John Carter Brown Library, Kathleen Wilson and the participants in the Coastlines program at SUNY Stony Brook, Tiffany Werth for arranging a keynote address I presented at the University of British Columbia, and the audience for a lecture at the Chicago Humanities Festival in 2013. These venues and others allowed me to benefit from the insights of a large number of scholars, including Maria Mavroudi, Michael Wintroub, Emily Berquist Soule, Ned Landsman, Jennifer Anderson, Nathalie Caron, Mary Fuller, Eric Slauter, Brad Bouley, Joanne Pillsbury, Strother Roberts, Chris Parsons, and Eric Hinderaker. I thank Erica Ginsburg for shepherding the book through the production process; my copy editor, Gillian Dickens; and Ericka Swensson, who helped with getting a grant from the Furthermore program of the J. M. Kaplan Fund, which supported the inclusion of the color plates. I thank too Cynthia Ingham, indexer *sans pareil*. And I am very pleased to be able to thank the archives that made images available, especially the Huntington Library, the John Carter Brown Library, and the Morgan Library, and of course the Mellon Foundation, which funded the lecture series.

In addition to the support from Penn, I received financial assistance from the Huntington, where I had an NEH/Huntington Fellowship in 2004–2005 and first began to explore the wonders of the "Vallard Atlas"; and the University of Southern California Undergraduate Research Assistant Program, which has provided me a stream of phenomenal student assistants. Of that group I want to especially thank Megan Hansford, Maddie Adams, Will Orr, Avery Wendell, and Emily Levine, all of them extraordinary at tracking down what must have seemed an endless number of documents and citations. In addition, I want to thank my colleagues at USC for their thoughtful interventions: Sherry Velasco, Amy Braden, Bill Deverell, Carole Shammas, Vanessa Schwartz, Nathan Perl-Rosenthal, Lindsay O'Neill, my former student Keith Pluymers, and especially Daniela Bleichmar, intrepid guide to all things visual in the early modern Atlantic basin. Amy Buono provided crucial information (and images) relating to sixteenth-century Brazil and the European encounter with Tupinambás. This book also would not exist without Lou Masur, Doug Greenberg, and Josh Piker, who along with Bob Lockhart provided the ongoing support to enable me to finish it.

In the end, even short books can have long pedigrees, and this is no exception. I thank the inspiration I received from Bernard Bailyn, who taught me how the Atlantic world came into existence, and Donald Worster, the most imaginative and perceptive environmental historian of our generation. For other kinds of inspiration I thank the entire Bitel, Mancall, Schoenberg, and Dunnous families, Sophie and Nicholas Mancall-Bitel, and of course Lisa Bitel, who gave this book whatever clarity and authority it possesses. And I dedicate this book to the memory of my parents, Elliott L. Mancall and Jacqueline C. Mancall, two scholars who were present for the original lectures, the last opportunity they had to hear me share my work.